Beat the Recession Marketing

Written By James Carley

A Real System designed to Help Small Businesses with BIG Visions Develop a Winning Marketing Strategy to Get MORE Customers, MORE Revenue and MORE Profits.

ISBN-13: 978-1481229692

CONTENTS

BEAT THE RECESSION MARKETING

SUCCESS MINDSET

Welcome to *Beat the Recession Marketing*. First off, I personally want to say thank you for taking the time to invest into this training. I promise that this course will definitely add value to your business and to your vision.

Before you get started, I want to say a few quick words that will help motivate and mentally prepare you. Learning something new is always exciting, especially if what you're learning will make a drastic change in your life. This book is that change.

So it's important going forward to have a mindset focused on success. Become a blank canvas. Remove defeat from your vocabulary and find the determination you need to do whatever it takes to succeed. Benjamin Franklin once said profoundly:

"Without continual growth and progress such words as improvement, achievement and success have no meaning"

Success for any business relies heavily on one key ingredient: **YOU**. Your mindset- not your friends', not your colleagues', not your family's- but **YOURS**. It's time to believe in yourself and in your abilities.

After years of real life experience in business, some success and some failures; I have realized that the timeless secret behind many successful entrepreneurs is the vast amount of determination, drive and perseverance they possess. A mindset focused on accomplishment and a heart dedicated to chasing their dreams.

Times are tough, so having an open mind to new knowledge will help open the door to a sea of endless opportunities. What this means is you must have a willingness to learn whatever it takes to be successful and then take massive **ACTION**.

If you study the common denominator of all the most successful men and women of the past or present, you will see this trait.

Understand that truly achieving success in your business is just a process, *NOT* a magic pill; but rather a series of real action steps taken daily that bring visibility, likability, and credibility to your business. You can never substitute good old fashion hard work with unrealistic processes.

So roll up your sleeves and get excited! You can do this. You're going to learn some effective marketing tactics combined to form a Multi-Channel Recession Blueprint. When you apply these tactics, you will strongly impact your business. Success starts today! Are you ready? Let's get started.

THE OPPORTUNITY

Every professional, regardless of the industry, has realized that times have changed. The side effects of a struggling economy and rapid technology advancement- such as **Smart Phones**, **Social Media** and **the Internet**- dramatically changed the way Americans connect with businesses.

This paradigm shift created the opportunity and need for this course.

If you've been in business for a while, most likely you've witnessed a huge drop in the effectiveness of **Traditional Outbound Marketing** response rates.

Everything from Yellow Pages™, Direct Mail, Radio, TV Commercials, and Flyers (*you name it*) has been affected by this shift. It raises two frequent questions that I'm asked daily from business owners and clients:

"Why is this happening" & "How do I fix this"?

The good news is that I'm going to show you both **WHY** and **HOW** throughout this course. I'll leave nothing to chance, but real action steps of what I actually do for my clients and personal projects.

I'm pretty frustrated with the amount of fluff and lack of value going around. The **backbone** of America is still Small Businesses. I want to do my part in helping rebuild our economy, one business at a time.

Currently, 97% of US Consumers now search online for information about a business or product **before** making a choice of doing business. This type of consumer behavior doesn't matter if a business is **online** or **offline**. Really think about this for a second.

The Internet has become the starting line where the "*Modern Consumer*" begins their purchasing experience; comparing prices, reading reviews, and trying to find the best deal possible, offered by the best company.

Top that off with the recent studies showing that for the first time in history- more people will be soon accessing the Internet via Mobile devices, rather than Desktop computers.

Suddenly, the platform where *Local Businesses* and *Local Consumers* meet is screaming for change. Now, what does this data and change in consumer behavior actually mean for business owners and entrepreneurs?

Simply that today's Modern Consumer is actively on- the- go. For a marketing plan in today's world to be successful, it must ***STOP*** interrupting what people are interested in and become **WHAT** people are interested in.

Here's a prime example. Have you ever been in the middle of watching a show on TV that you really wanted to watch and it was interrupted by the infamous "*Special News Report*" about the latest trending topic?

Now at that exact moment you're ready to jump into the TV and turn into Muhammad Ali- LOL! You just want to watch your show, right?

But imagine during your favorite show, that same trending topic was talked about. You would be more inclined to **remember it** and more inclined to **take action**. Why? Stop to ask yourself.

It's because the marketing message didn't interrupt what you were doing, but coincided within it. The obvious days of pushy marketing are over. I want you to realize something: You see this tactic in play every day, but probably aren't even aware of it.

Think about when you're using Google™ and you see the PPC Ads on the side or when you're using Facebook™ and the PPC Ads are also on the side. These are prime examples of this genius principal at work.

By reaching consumers "**where they are**" on channels- such as *Mobile, Social*, and *Local*- you can stop interrupting consumers active lifestyle and start engaging them.

Focus on building real relationships that continue to nurture prospects from Leads to Fans into Customers. This is done through a strategic sales funnel process that combines:

<u>Local</u> + <u>Mobile</u> + <u>Social Media Strategies</u>

Your marketing plan should never consist of single tactics, like Facebook™, SEO, Yellow Pages™, Emails, Mailers and so on. These things do work when used correctly, but **<u>before</u>** you start these, you first need to have a System (***plan***) in place.

You need a powerful system that's based on a Multi-Channel Marketing strategy that reaches modern consumers where they are and speaks their language; directly infusing your marketing message to grab consumers' attention.

A Unique Sales Funnel is where you can:

1. Increase Leads
2. Capture Leads
3. Nurture Leads (*engage*)
4. Increase Conversions
5. Increase Retention
6. Build a Reputation

My goal is to help change your perspective about how you go about getting sales. Here's why, let me ask you a serious question.

Think about all the current marketing you're doing and all the traffic your marketing brings- **NOT** sales, just traffic (*eyeballs and walk-ins*).

What are you doing with the visitors who **ARE** interested, but they ***DON'T*** buy or do anything? Chances are you don't even know who they are!

Recent statistics show that "*Only 1.1% of first-time visitors' results in a new sale*". Seriously, think of all the traffic that comes to your website or your place of business.

This traffic includes all the window shoppers, freebie seekers and everyone else who has shown interest but doesn't buy right away. What are you doing with them?

Statistics continue to show that 98% of all traffic that leaves your business never returns. So where are they going? They're probably going to your competition.

Really stop to think about this. How many people do you talk to or come in contact with before someone buys? Quite a few, correct?

See, you must expose customers to your brand's message over and over again for them to realize and internalize it. Every marketing message sent out today must be socially relevant; attached with a great customer experience.

In order to get more sales and improve your profit, you can't "*put your hope*" into making a sale to the first time visitor. If you do- great, but you still need to put a system in place.

You need a System that **STOPS** Leads from "*falling thru the cracks*", instead of wasting your precious advertising dollars and gives up too soon.

Get ready because this is exactly what you're going to gain from this book, piece by piece, until you understand completely; what to do concluded with an Action Plan Blueprint.

OVERVIEW AND OBJECTIVE

What you're going to learn inside this book is a Complete Marketing System. No theory, no fluff, but a real system, Developed and Centered on a Multi-Channel Strategy.

Multi-Channel Marketing is marketing using many different marketing channels to "*reach*" a customer.

For most businesses, a marketing channel might be a retail location, website, social network, mail order catalog or direct personal communications like emails, text messages, or a letter.

The objective of the companies doing this type of marketing is to make it easy for consumers to buy from them in anyway, that they feel comfortable.

Our System is designed to give your business the formula to an effective, targeted, Recession Proof Marketing plan; *a realistic powerful solution to any marketing dilemmas*.

My main objective and focus is to truly help you Beat the Recession in the middle of an economic crisis. I want you to grow your business and produce enough **Profit** and **Revenue** to seriously impact your local community.

By your business implementing my gorilla style marketing strategy, you will see results delivered fast and consistently.

I'm leaving nothing to chance inside this book. Rather, I'm revealing absolutely everything you need to properly connect with consumers and grow your business. Eliminate all your current frustration by learning something new that will make a huge difference inside your business.

My Strategy Consists of 6 Pillars: *Your Website, Mobile, Social Media, Email, Video* and *Off-line*.

The purpose of these pillars are to help you create visibility, increase engagement, and communicate with consumers on their "*preferred channel*" of choice; teaching you a better more effective way to get attention.

By not interrupting consumers' daily activities, but rather drawing interested prospects into a Unique Sales Funnel, you will be able to:

1. Educate
2. Entertain
3. Capture
4. Convert
5. Follow Up

This will systematically make it easier for your business to consistently get new customers (*leads*) and retain them, while building strong customer retention.

This system will teach you exactly how to provide solutions to customer's needs, wants, problems and questions.

Now, this may sound like a lot of work, but don't worry- you can do this! Real results require a real plan. "***Businesses that fail to plan can only plan to fail***".

Once you get set up and running, your business will have a full Lead Generation and Retention System, that will cut your marketing budget in half.

Plus our system provides the ability to measure your marketing ROI in immense detail; making sure your business marketing plan is both airtight and realistic for today's modern consumer.

Notes

_____

_____

_____

_____

_____

_____

_____

_____

_____

_____

_____

_____

_____

_____

_____

_____

_____

_____

_____

UNDERSTAND YOUR MARKET

When you're in the beginning building stages of developing a business marketing plan, it's very important that you first identify and understand your market. Becoming what the market needs and providing valued packed solutions doesn't happen by accident.

This stage requires a scientific approach that will properly layout the pieces needed to gain detailed market insight. There are 4 major elements that you must know and understand before you can formulate a Recession-Proof Marketing strategy.

1. Who Are Your Ideal Customers
2. Your Competition's Activities
3. Your Customer Needs
4. Your Main Objective – (of starting your campaign)

Do you know WHO your "Ideal Customers" are?

1. What Their Needs Are?
2. How Old They Are?
3. Likes and Interests?
4. Their Pain Points?
5. Their Frustrations?
6. Types of Content They Actively Consume?

Then how will you know what to sell and whom to sell too? See, there is a huge myth going around that I would like to clear up. The myth states: **"Everyone is Your Customer"**.

This Simply is *NOT* the case. Marketing is about getting your targeted message in front of targeted consumers. Your marketing message must speak their language and be targeted precisely for your Ideal Customer.

For example, let's say the Ideal Customer of your product or service is a 30 year old mother of 3 and she wants a reliable four-door car for the family because they have outgrown their two-door and need more space. But your marketing messages **automatically** are trying to sell her a two-door sports car. Obviously, from the beginning, she's not going to be interested because it doesn't match (*connect*) with her core needs and wants, right?

But imagine if you already knew that she wanted a four-door car for her family. It would be an **INSTANT** attraction and connection because you tailored the marketing conversation for that Ideal Customer's needs.

The main objective in this scenario is to sell the car, but *not* any car- the one the customer needs.

How do you know what her needs are? Because you have done your **homework** and can relate to who she is, what questions are on her mind, and any possible interests that she may have. It's all about **Relationship Marketing**.

BUYING PROCESS

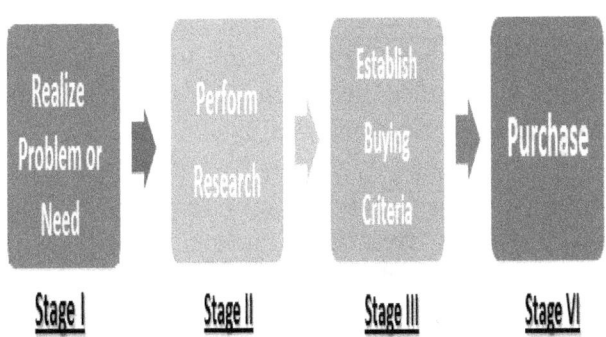

Realize Problem or Need	Perform Research	Establish Buying Criteria	Purchase
Stage I	Stage II	Stage III	Stage VI

Magic happens when you put the customer first. Please stay with me- this is important. The reason you want to do this is to understand what's called the "**Buying Process**".

The buying process simply means the psychology behind **why** and **how** consumers go about buying things. There's a series of "*physical steps*" people take before they buy anything.

This process is behind why people walk into your business, call your office and buy your products or services. Let's breakdown how the consumer Buying Process works in detail, so you can clearly understand the need for creating an Optimized Sales Process.

Stage I – A customer realizes a problem, want, or need, then immediately begins searching for a solution (*Google™, Social Media, Review Sites, Friends, Word-of-Mouth, Advertisements*).

Stage II – While performing research, they begin to understand their options and possible solutions.

Stage III – Next, they begin to decide what present companies meet their personal criteria and have the best prices and quality.

Stage IV – Lastly, they're now ready to buy and are looking for free trials, discounts, coupons, or demos to seal the deal.

I want you to notice how extremely powerful these Stages are. Once you fully understand and know WHO your Ideal Customers are, you can **identify** the actual STEPS they take to buy your products and services.

You will then use this data to create a "*Custom Sales Funnel*" that greets prospects systematically in every stage of that *Buying Process*. From the beginning of the Sales Process (***Front End***) to the end of the Sales Cycle (***Back End***), you must have a system (***plan***) in place to capture, engage, and convert prospects.

Great job! I know this was some pretty meaty content. I'm very proud of you for making it through. Now that you understand why having a plan is essential for success, let's dive into how to identify your markets "***Ideal Customer***".

MARKET ANALYSIS

In the last section, you learned how the buying process works. All that's left is researching your market and identifying <u>who</u> your Ideal Customers are- then figuring out <u>what</u> needs they have and <u>what</u> they're looking for.

Painting this picture makes things easier as you develop your markets "*Customer Avatar*". You can do this using many free tools online, but the two main tools I love to use are:

1. Google Keyword Tool™
2. Quantcast™

The Google Free Keyword Tool™, if you don't already know, keeps track of the search queries entered into <u>Google.com</u>.

Nowadays, whenever someone is looking for something *Online* or *Offline*, they break out their Smart Phone and Google it. Google™ today is like having the Yellow Pages™ combined with an ultra-thin encyclopedia in your pocket.

The amazing thing is that Google™ records all this data for future use inside their Adwords™ campaigns, which is their paid advertising platform. Having access to this search information saves us years of doing customer surveys and detailed report analysis ourselves; revealing the needs and mind of our market directly to us.

We are going to leverage this data **NOT** from a SEO perspective. But rather to get a better understanding of how **BIG** our market is and what exactly people are looking for within that market. Remember, we're putting the consumer first and adding real value that will build positive relationships.

So for example let's say I was a Local Restaurant Owner in San Diego, CA. Now this could be any profession, any product or service, and I wanted to see just how many people were looking for me. All I would have to do is enter my Keyword *(phrase I want to be recognized fo*r) directly into the Google Keyword Tool™ and hit search.

All the information returned is PROOF positive of the number of times (*monthly*) people **Offline** are turning to **Online**. These keywords are code words for your market has a problem or need.

If you ever wanted to know if there is a **demand** for your company's products or services "*now you know*". Once you know for a fact that people are looking for you, next is using the power of Google™ to determine the size of that market.

You can do this by just making sure the "**Sort by Relevancy**" filter is on. Then you're going to use a sharp business eye to look for certain keywords that closely relate to your business. Next you want to take the mouse and select those keywords that closely relate to your business then export them to a CSV file.

Once that file is downloaded, open the file and add up each *local search volume* together. The grand total represents how **big** or **small** your market currently is and any online search interest according to the search engines.

Now you may be asking yourself what's the point of this? The point is when it comes to a marketing campaign knowing if it's worth:

- o Spending money to acquire new customers
- o How much you should spend on marketing
- o What type of promo offers to offer prospects
- o What type of devices are people using

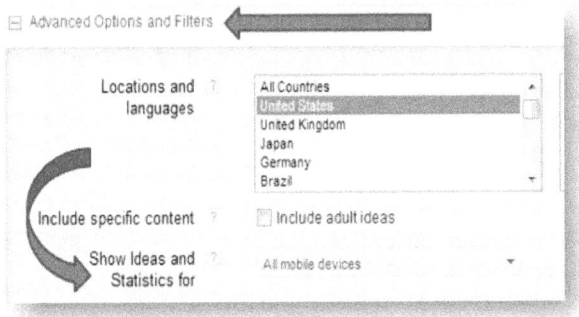

This last part is really cool. Finding what *type of devices* are people using to find you. Go back to your Google Keyword Tool™ results and click the "**Advanced Options and Filters**".

On the drop-down menu click "**Show Ideas and Statistics For**" then choose **All Mobile Devices,** then click search.

Google™ will take your same chosen keywords and display how many searches are coming from a mobile device. I suggest downloading and using the "**Market Keyword Evaluation Form**" (*CSV file*) I've created for you in the resource section. Then combine this insider data with all your other keyword numbers from earlier, so you have both.

These results are important because it indicates that you need to have both a *Desktop* and *Mobile* Website or Landing Page for your marketing campaigns; so you never miss an opportunity for new business.

This little optimization tweak could increase sales conversions by 10 to 15% minimal just by being mobile friendly. Stop to ask yourself how does my Website look on a mobile phone? Review the total search volume for your market and see the percentage of consumers who are mobile users.

Tip to remember about the Google keyword Tool™:

These numbers aren't 100% exact. You can filter between exact match or phrase to get best case and worst case scenario. Don't make this too deep. You're just using this information to determine that people are looking for you and there is a market for what you're trying to offer.

Now that you know what the Google Keyword Tool™ can do. Here's how you use the tool to determine the **needs**, **wants** and **questions** inside your market. This is where majority of businesses rush and do things backwards, making it very hard on themselves.

Normal Business Start Up

Let's say for example there's a business woman named "*Susan*". She operates a popular family owned bakery in her local community. One day Susan has a great idea to revolutionize fruitcakes by turning them into cupcakes.

Next, she asked her friends and family what they think. Most of them liked the idea and others loved it. Susan then decided to bring that idea to **LIFE**.

Then Susan took out a loan and borrowed money to invest into her idea. Finally once her business launched, she soon realizes the demand for her product isn't quite there, resulting in few sales.

Why did this happen?

Q: Because her idea wasn't good? - **No**
Q: Because people didn't want what she had to offer? - **No**

Q: Because she didn't properly understand or study the market? - **Yes**

Here's the eye-opener. Often times we ask our family, colleagues and friends what they think about our ideas. This is fine- nothing wrong with asking the people closest to us.

But you have to remember your friends and family are **NOT** your Ideal Customers. They may buy from you, support you, but when it comes to business they're not your "*Targeted Market*".

In other words, just because you have a great idea doesn't mean there is a market for it. That's why it's crucial before starting any campaign you must do your homework.

This is critical so you don't try to force feed the market, something they don't want. Doing this saves both time and money, not including the stress from having a failed marketing campaign.

Next, to determine the needs of your market you must get inside the mind of your customer. Think like them, really placing yourself in their shoes. Remember we're putting the customer before the sale.

In order for us to create high valued products and services that answers their questions or solves their problems, this is mandatory. Creating quality of this kind is what keeps customers coming back, telling their friends about you and becoming loyal customers.

The way to accomplish this is making a list of:

- o Questions they might have about your products or services?
- o What problems do your products or services solve?
- o What industry questions about your profession are people wondering?

You can do this easily by doing a little data research.

- o Visit Related Blogs (*look at topics and comments*)
- o Visit Forums (*look at popular threads discussions*)
- o Just Think Out-Of-The-Box (*everywhere socially*)

I've also included a custom **Market Questions and Needs Locator** form download located in the resource section that you can enter keywords onto. Build a relevant list of possible questions and wants of your market.

Then after you have a list of market keywords go back to the Google Keyword Tool™ and see the local search volume behind those questions, needs and buyer keywords.

Remember always to check how many local mobile searches they are and save them to your CSV file for future marketing campaign usage.

Here's an extra golden nugget. If you would like to dig deeper there's another great tool that Google™ offers called *Google Insights™*. This tool is extremely powerful, especially if you run a local business.

Insights shows you exactly where your customers are geographically and any fresh rising search terms that people are looking for.

This is very similar to Google Keyword Tool™ and works in conjunction with it. This is great for staying on top of your market and discovering any new keywords or recognizing rising social trends.

Everyone, please remember our greatest asset in this whole equation is our **BRAIN**, not the tools. Finding ways to create value really pays off when the customer **LOVES** your products or services.

This type of natural social proof reveals you honestly care about the customer and that's really what its marketing is all about "*the relationship*".

IDENTIFY YOUR IDEAL CUSTOMER

After identifying the needs, questions and pain points of your ideal market; it's imperative to understand what the real person behind computer looks like.

Meaning you need to develop a "crystal ball" insight about the consumer who's looking for solutions to the problems you found during the *Market Analysis* stage.

This information combined with your market data will provide all the pieces needed to properly speak the "**language**" of the consumer. Allowing you to easily grab their attention and charge your marketing campaigns with extreme value. Let's dive right into the training.

The first step you want take is going online to Quantcast.com. Quantcast™ is the industry leading Web Analytics platform that examines and ranks millions of websites.

Quantcast™ is an extremely powerful, free and easy to operate tool that provides incredible value. During this process your main objective is to take a detailed look into the **TYPE** of traffic your competition receives online. Next open a Second browser window and go to Google™.

These two sites together are what I call your **"Consumer Dashboard"**. The amount of useful data you can extract from these two sites alone can help position your campaigns for success (*used correctly*).

Once you're on Google™, enter in your main keyword from your list or any phrase you want to be recognized for. Next from the results copy the top five organic results page URLs and paste them into Quantcast.com one by one. I've also created for you a "**Customer Social Profile**" form to record all your data (*located in resources section*).

The idea behind this step is 9 out of 10 times these top sites found in Google™ are your direct competition. These sites are receiving majority of the traffic displayed in the Google Keyword Tool™.

Remember success leaves clues right? Reverse engineering the top sites and further analyzing these sites who are receiving all this traffic, will help us paint a detailed picture of what our ideal customer really looks like.

After you enter each competitor Website URL into Quantcast.com and hit search. The following screen will reveal basic traffic information. What you're interested in is the two tabs on the right side that point out the visitors *Demographics* and *Lifestyle* a.k.a. Psychographics.

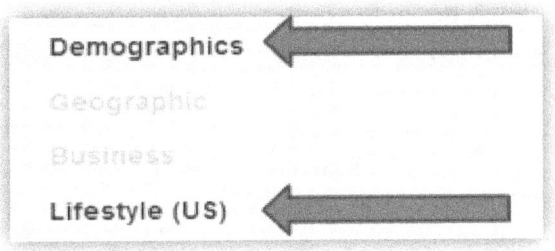

Psychographics in short, pay attention to the lifestyle, attitude and behavior behind a person to help form a more detailed picture of who they are.

This is why many social networks ask about your likes and dislikes when you sign up. Information of this caliber makes it easier to segment and target users for future marketing messages.

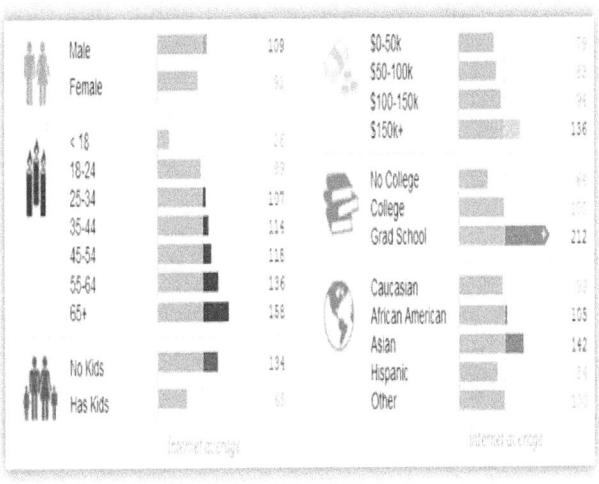

Next, click on the Demographics tab. On this page you can see a record of all the visitors that peculiar site gets. Better yet, you can see the person behind the computer. Kind of cool, huh?

You now have a crystal clear image about who the ideal visitor is to this website: their gender, age, children, household income, education level and ethnicity.

Can you see how extremely powerful this insider information will be for the success of your future marketing campaigns?

Now what you want to do is repeat this process for the remaining four sites; recording all your findings on the "**Customer Social Profile form**".

During this process, make sure to keep an eye out for any correlating data between competing sites and highlight any similarities that standout.

Often times during this process we discover many golden nuggets that help advance our campaigns greatly.

It's important to remember that all we're using this online data for is to create *targeted marketing messages* to use during your campaigns. The main point of relationship marketing is to always speak the language of the customer. This is simply that process at work.

The fact of the matter is we all have been witness of this type of message targeting before- whether you know it or not. For example, have you ever seen a commercial or read a slogan that screamed "*that's me*"? Then once the commercial was over you thought to yourself "*I need or want that*". Honestly, sure you have, we all have! This is not by accident.

Results like this are from a business knowing exactly WHO their targeted market is and simply giving them what they're asking for; this is a demonstration of supply and demand in motion.

What I just showed you is on the surface level. You can dig much deeper by using different web and social analytics tools, but this will help you shape majority of your campaigns.

There's also Google Ad Planner™, which is an awesome free tool that works in conjunction with Quantcast.com- but either one works just fine.

Knowing the markets wants and what your Ideal Customer looks like provides ultimate consumer accuracy. Marketing success relies heavily upon your message and knowing who you're targeting.

Take this formula and apply it to your business. Start engaging consumers with your marketing material because your content is quality and speaks directly to their needs.

Notes

_____

_____

_____

_____

_____

_____

_____

_____

_____

_____

_____

_____

_____

_____

_____

_____

_____

_____

_____

_____

_____

KNOWING YOUR COMPETITION

The core strength of any business comes from a proper understanding of knowing "*who they are*" in the market place. What current position do you hold when compared to your competition?

What exactly are their strengths and weaknesses stacked against your strengths and weaknesses? Whose value proposition out delivers the rest in the consumer's eye? How are consumers socially engaging with their marketing efforts?

These are questions you must answer to determine the strength of your competition and better entry into the market. The last element needed to fully construct your markets "**Customer Avatar**".

No one goes into battle without knowing who they are up against. This is our process required to gather quality Market Intel. You started learning about this process in the last module, so let's go over some points you covered.

Quick Recap: *(you want to)*

- o Search Google™ using our Top Keywords
- o Recognize the Top 10 Results as Competition
- o Remember these 10 Sites receive the Search Engine Traffic found in the Google™

So the first thing you want to do is open your **Competition Website Analysis / Social Analysis** form (*spread sheet located in resource section*). Taking notes at this stage is crucial.

We're going to reverse engineer in-depth how your competition is presenting themselves to the market place. Jotting down any similarities or major impacts they're doing to become more visible to consumers.

During this *Competition Analysis* we're going to breakdown the process into two separate sections: **Website Analysis** and **Social Analysis**. Both present a unique perspective needed to help you understand the strength of your competition.

You're going to use some free tools and your brain to look at how competitors' websites:

1. Are Graphically Designed
2. Are Optimized and Structured
3. How They're Doing Socially
4. How Viral is Their Website and Content
5. Types of Channels are Consumers Engaging
6. Types of Content Formats are Being Shared Socially

The purpose of segmenting this information is remembering that "**success leaves clues**". Every business that is successful today has put in the **HARD** work to get there.

You simply want to recognize those clues and emulate that success to grow your business. Stop trying to reinvent the wheel and get innovative, using what's already proven to work.

Grab your pen and let's start analyzing the facts responsible for your competition's success in the market place.

Website Analysis

A Website should be a powerful asset in your company's arsenal that works hard for you twenty four hours a day. Providing a digital channel to sell your products, services and educating people about your company.

Business professionals spend a lot of money to make sure their Company Website is optimized and structured correctly for consumers. Creating a great user experience that draws visitors over and over again isn't by accident, but rather a well-oiled plan of attack designed for both **Search Engines** and **Consumers**.

We're going to take a look behind the curtain to see how your competition sets themselves apart and became popular (*visible*) in the community; creating your company's own detailed **marketing audit** of each Top Ranking Popular Website in your market.

The point of this is to look for any similarities and correlating data between competing sites. This information will reveal to you vital **instructions** of what to do or what not to do. This is closely related to the "Barrier of Entry" into a market or things that must be done to be seen competitive.

The first thing you want to do is grab your data spreadsheet of the Top Ranking Competing sites from **Understanding Your Market** stage. Then start visiting the sites individually on your list.

One of the quickest ways to do this is using a free tool called **Traffic Travis™** (*or any similar tool*). Remember, we're not using this for any kind of SEO purpose, but rather to get a better visual representation and understanding of your current Competitions Website Optimization.

There are 4 Main Factors you want to look at using this tool. Factors include:

1. Is the Main Keyword being used in the Title of the page? (*Shows how people are finding them via search engines*)
2. Are they using a Keyword in their URL? (*Another indication that they're targeting this keyword on purpose*)
3. The Google Page Rank™ given to that page? (*Shows if Google actually views this site as an Authority*)
4. How many Backlinks are going to that page? (*Shows the number of people sharing and talking about this sites content*)

After you look at these factors, you're going to take a closer look at each site manually to identify a few more factors. So take a few minutes to visit the first site from your list and scroll around the site. See how effectively they're communicating and engaging with consumers.

Behaviors to Look For:

1. Are they using Videos, Images or Articles? (***Shows engagement types***)
2. Is their Website Modern and Up-To-Date? (***Shows how visually users would be attracted to their brand***)
3. Do you see Lead Capture Forms or Site Pop Ups? (***Shows if they're building a List of targeted prospects***)
4. What Types of Irresistible Offers are they giving customers? (***Shows what kind of offers to create, emulate and make better***)
5. Is there a Mobile Website Version of their site? (***Shows they're paying attention to their customers user experience***

All the results from the Website Analysis paint a clear road map of what you need to do with your Website.

These are the main elements you must complete in order to outrank your competition online or offline. Especially when it comes to: *Being Easily Found inside Search Engines, Becoming Visual appealing, Providing Great Offers or Specials, Capturing Leads Fast and Easily* while providing the Ultimate User Experience. These are huge factors that can't be ignored. Next we're going to continue putting the pieces together with our Social Analysis.

Social Analysis

In today's reputation economy Social Media has become the new **Word-Of-Mouth**. The internet has given everyone a platform to share their voice and opinion with the world.

This doorway used correctly can position your company directly into the heart of internet conversation.

During this 2nd step inside "**Knowing Your Competition**" you're going to learn how to properly analyze every major Social Media channel; to determine where exactly online your competition's content is being Shared, Liked, and Tweeted.

When your website or content is shared socially, this indicates to Consumers and Search Engines there's value "*here*". Normally, the higher value you present to the market place helps positions your brands authority.

The more you increase authority during this stage the chances of your website or content going viral dramatically increases. If your business succeeds at the task of going viral, everything you know changes almost instantly. Literally overnight your business could go from blending in (*invisible*) to standing out. Creating all the Social-Proof needed to establish your businesses social credibility.

Producing a good amount of high quality, useful or engaging content for consumers will also drive traffic online and offline.

Here are some of the top sites to examine while performing a Social Analysis:

1. Facebook™
2. Twitter™
3. Google Plus™
4. Yelp™
5. Pinterest™
6. LinkedIn™ *(& more depending on Industry)*

Content deemed valuable to users draws a lot of attention. Especially when the content helps consumers decide which product or service best fits their needs.

For this reason you need to see which of your competitors websites and pieces of content are being shared socially the most. There are many ways to do this both *Free* and *Paid*.

Here is a **FREE** Tool Example (I've included a paid recommendation for both Website and Social Analysis in the resource section). But for this FREE example let's go to a new awesome site called Sharedcount.com.

Once you're there you will have the option to add the URLs of your Top Competition Sites. Use the same Keywords and URL's you found during the **"Understanding Your Market"** stage. Once all the URL's are entered press search to start the examination process.

The results provide a clear breakdown exactly how many times each individual URL has been mentioned on multiple Social Networks. Take your time and really examine the results. They reveal very important information needed for your upcoming campaigns. Next download and save a CSV copy of the report. Then add this data to your **Competition Website Analysis & Social Analysis** form.

Use this information to plan out:

1. Your Contents Voice
2. Your Content Type (*Article, Video, etc.*)
3. What Social Sites to Focus Sharing Content On
4. How Well to Optimize Social Channels (*Postings, Landing Pages, etc.*).

This is good stuff guys. By now, you've learned almost everything about your customer. Next you're going to learn how to take ALL this data and create your markets **"Customer Avatar"**. Putting an actual face to your customer makes marketing very transparent and increases overall campaign effectiveness.

CUSTOMER AVATAR

You have learned that achieving success in any online or offline marketing campaign drastically depends on proper message targeting.

The ability to identify your ideal audience from the masses is like finding a buried treasure- a beautiful diamond in the rough. Let me explain.

During the "*Understanding Your Market*" and "*Knowing Your Competition*" early stages, you gathered all data needed to create an effective marketing plan.

Taking all the necessary steps to properly analyze your true competition's recent online and social activity, to point out what's next.

Here's where the magic happens. We're going to structure all this information to formulate your markets "**Customer Avatar**".

Painting a crystal-clear picture about everything you know about your "*Ideal Customer*" thus far; provides you the perfect outline that will shape **WHAT** your ideal customer really looks like.

Using the San Diego Restaurant example from earlier, Our Ideal Customer looks like: (*remember to replace with your own market data*).

Demographics
- 30 Years Old
- Female
- Married
- 3 Kids

Social Behavior
- Interest 1
- Interest 2
- Has Facebook
- Uses Mobile

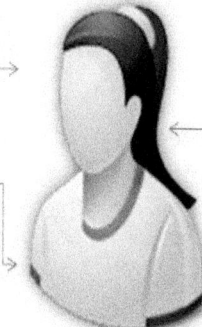

Content & Offers
- Videos
- Articles
- Images
- Coupons

Demographics:

1. 30 Years Old
2. Female
3. Married
4. Has 3 Kids
5. Makes $30K a Year
6. Somewhat Educated

Social Behaviors:

1. Has Interest in humor
2. Also Interested in fashion
3. Has Facebook, Google, Twitter Accounts
4. Actively Reads Reviews
5. Uses Local Mobile Search

Content Types and Offers:

1. Watches Videos
2. Reads Articles
3. Likes Images
4. Likes Family Coupons
5. Likes 10% off Discounts

Conclusion:

After reviewing all the data, you can say our Ideal Customer "*Susan*" for example, (*insert any name*) is a married middle aged female, who has 3 kids and works full time with little formal education.

She really enjoys humor and fashion. Socially, she actively uses Facebook™, Google Plus™, and Twitter™ to stay connected to friends. She reads business reviews on her Smartphone (*mobile*) and watches online videos. She loves quality articles with images that provide some type of bargain, especially deals that offer good coupons or family discounts.

Can you recognize my perspective on how to put together all the pieces (*data*)? Wow! This stuff is extremely powerful when it's put into action! Hopefully you realize by now what separates a successful company from the pack.

A business today achieves success for a **REAL** reason. Once you have done your homework, you can clearly see the clues success leaves. No magic pill, just old fashion **HARD** work.

This is **WHY** majority of businesses fail. Because majority of them **DONT** have a plan in place and without one, you can only plan to fail. So it's crucial to have a system in place that works for you, *Knows Your Customer, Generates Leads, Engages Prospects* and *Converts*.

Next I'm going teach you how to structure my Multi-Channel *"6 Pillar Marketing System"*. It's guaranteed to reach customers "**where they are**" and to deliver quality information they want-increasing visibility while strategically getting the word out about your business. When this system is implemented you will create a **Custom Sales Funnel** designed especially for your Company's Ideal Customer.

INTRO TO FUNNEL SYSTEM

It's time to put on your game face. You are now entering "The Meat" of the whole program. This is what you've been waiting for.

So get excited, because in these next few modules you're going to learn how to setup and implement my *Beat the Recession Marketing* Strategy!

A winning system designed to put your business in the driver's seat, connecting you directly with your targeted consumer.

Teaching your business how to become what people want, while delivering what they need, by introducing a step by step process for creating your company's own Unique Sales Funnel.

Formulating this Sales Funnel is based on all the data you've learned during the "***Understanding Your Market***" and "***Customer Avatar***" training.

I'm revealing my *6 Pillar System* that will show you how to structure well optimized and targeted communication channels.

These channels (*when setup correctly*) will draw customers into a single Sales Funnel in real time, delivering real measurable results.

This is centered on a Multi-Channel Marketing strategy, which creatively combines and leverages multiple marketing channels to reach a customer.

This type of marketing reaches consumers "*where they are*", making it incredible easy for businesses to directly communicate with consumers on their **"preferred channel"** of choice.

Here are 5 major benefits that implementing my Beat the Recession strategy will produce.

Increase Your Visibility in the Marketplace: The state of today's marketplace is noisy with so many offers. Customers are overwhelmed by all the marketing messages thrown at them daily. You're going to learn how to stand out, be unique and provide real solutions to everyday problems, while building a *5 STAR Reputation* that will shorten your sales process.

Generate Interested Leads: The life blood of every business is New Customers. But reaching customers where they are is no easy task. You're going to learn how to setup and optimize the most effective marketing channels; that will position your business presence where it matters the most, making it easy for consumers to connect with your company's irresistible offers.

Capture Leads & Engage Them: The strongest asset any business has is their customer database. Building a list of interested prospects allows you to nurture (*build up*) the relationship into a sale. You're going to learn how to setup and optimize all your marketing materials (*online & offline*) to encourage prospects to take action.

Convert Fans into Sales: The single most important metric that can double a company's bottom-line is your Conversion Rates. Making the most of each lead your business receives will help skyrocket return on investment goals. You're going to learn how setup and fully maximize your current marketing channels performance, sending conversion rates where they can be felt "*Your Pocket*".

Build Customer Retention: Did you know it's five times cheaper to reactive a previous customer then acquiring a new customer? Not including previous customers will buy more from you because trust has already been established. You're going to learn strategies how to leverage your past relationships and turn them into a profit, keeping customers coming back for more and more.

Now stay focused and take notes, this information will change your business; providing you much needed insight to satisfy the wants and needs of your market. It's very important going forward (*2013 & beyond*) that business owners and entrepreneurs begin to start **THINKING** like a marketer.

Understand that having a real marketing plan is not an option, but rather a necessity: the price of doing business, **NOT** a liability for your business.

The impact of having a marketing plan in place makes such a **BIG** difference to your bottom-line. Short term goals to long term, just having one simply makes sense. So strap yourself in, lock the doors and dive into the material.

At the end of the training make sure to download the **Beat the Recession Blueprint PDF**, and then watch my FREE Bonus Videos on **"What's My Reputation"** and **"Why 2 Go Mobile"** located in the resource section.

PILLAR #1: YOUR WEBSITE

Welcome to Pillar #1 "*Your Website*". In this module you're going to learn some very powerful strategies that will help optimize your website for maximum conversions.

By maximizing your site for conversions allows you to save money on advertising while creating a better quality user experience. Simply because you're making the most out of each visitor (*lead*) your site receives.

Everyone knows your website acts as the "*face*" of your business, a digital extension of your company's voice. Often times your website is the first point of contact prospects see when learning about your business. So it's very important you make the first impression a professional one.

Now thinking back to how the consumer buying process works, what is the first thing a consumer does after they consciously realize they have a want or problem? Do you remember? That's right, 97% of them search online.

So whether they came across your website via:

1. Google™
2. Social Media
3. Off-line Advertising

You must make sure your website presents you as an industry leader. Consumers are looking for real solutions to their problems, needs and wants. Does your website provide answers to their questions? Are you presenting real solutions to their problems? If you're **NOT**, the competition is.

Let's dive into a few ways that you can optimize your website to capture and engage leads, making the conversion process easy and rewarding for consumers; honestly keeping them satisfied is our main objective.

Design: The first element we're going to take a look at on your website is *"Website design"*.

Your website design must be:

1. Up-to-date (*with Relevant Content*)
2. Modern (*Latest Technology, CMS, etc.*)
3. Visually Appealing (*For multiple of reasons*)

Imagine when you first met a business person and they said they were a Top Lawyer in San Diego for example. But he or she had an unprofessional appearance. What are the chances you would **TRUST** them to represent you in court and earn your business?

Slim, right? But, why?

Because first impressions and appearances **DO** count; it helps visually to position yourself as an expert, not only in person but online as well. Often times many people associate value with appearance. Like the saying goes "*never judge a book by its cover*". Unfortunately most people **DO**. So make sure your website is up-to-date.

Relevancy: The next element you want to look at is being "Relevancy".

What this means is making sure the information your **"Ideal Customer"** wants is located on your website; this includes any product and service questions, market updates, insider tips or product details; in other words, being in "**tune**" with your market.

These are the steps necessary to becoming a real **"Authority"** in your market; a true one-stop-shop for all your customers' needs. Providing the best Quality Content in your market is the real goal here.

Ways to Be Found Relevant:

1. Interesting Articles
2. Engaging Videos
3. Blog Posts
4. Info-graphics
5. Press Release, etc.

Any possible relevant information that your target

audience would deem useful; doing this will help build trust within your market and customers.

Increasing both user engagement and interactivity with your sites content encourages consumers to share what they liked socially. This will help build credibility within the search engines and establish all the social proof needed to shorten your overall sales process.

Lead Capturing: The second to last element in this module is *"Lead Capture"*.

Lead Capturing is something most of us are very familiar with but never actually do, or have a *HARD* time implementing. The important fact to remember is the money is always in the "**List**" (*customer database*).

This vastly popular cardinal rule applies to every business model. Honestly if there was ONE single element that would impact your business the most its building a list.

There are hundreds of Million dollar to Billion dollar companies whose entire business model is based solely on receiving revenue from the *relationship with their customer database.*

For instance companies like *Groupon*™ and other daily deal sites generate leads for local businesses strictly from their own list, then turnaround and charge local businesses for access to their list.

The amazing thing is statistics show daily deal sites are expected to double there revenue 100% each year. A 100% increase! This speaks volumes of what building a list can do. Even during a recession.

Understand the benefit of building your own customer database is like having the ability to print money on demand. Similar to how a squirrel stores away his acorns (*customers*) for future use. Anytime he needs an acorn, he has a supply. If ever there's a drought (*slow business*) he's ok.

I cannot express how extremely powerful this is. Imagine having a direct (*instant*) connection with your customers, forming healthy communication channels that drive interested leads to any bargain or deal that you might have.

The best way to Capture Leads that visit your website is making sure your site has Some type of:

1. Optin Form (*pop up, content embed or widget*)
2. Optin Page (*squeeze/landing page*)

Now you can have an Optin Page on more than your website but we'll talk about that in later modules. Providing your customers a way to hear about all the cool things going on in your business drives Optins.

Please understand this is something consumers really want, and is a HUGE asset to you. Make sure your website has some type of "Lead Capture System" in place.

Shareability: Okay, the last element we're going to talk about for your Website is *"Shareability"*.

We all know about the serious viral power that Social Networks present. Installing various social icons on your website allows customers to share those quality videos or articles on your site easily with friends.

This is simple but highly effective- a vital piece for expanding your visibility and credibility in the marketplace.

Just make sure every page and blog post has its own way to be shared virally, depending on the type of website you have HTML or Wordpress. This is very easy to do. Usually this only requires installing a social plugin or embedding code into the desired page.

Remember to have call-to-actions on your website that encourage people to share your content with their friends.

Recap:

So let's do a quick recap of what you learned in *Pillar #1*.

Design: You learned how having a modern, up-to-date and relevant website helps represent your company professionally and makes the first impression count.

Relevant: Next you learned how being found relevant by providing quality content, helps position you to become an authority in your market; showing that you truly understand customer's needs.

Lead Capture: Then you learned the hidden power behind building a customer database and why having a list is the single biggest asset your business can have.

Shareability: Finally you learned how allowing visitors to share socially your Websites content will dramatically increase popularity through social proof aka *"New Aged PR"*.

Homework:

Your homework from this module is to examine your website and take a look at these *4 Elements*. Make sure your website has them in place. If not it's time for some adjustments.

Looking at your competition helps see what other possible elements you need to improve on and do better. Helping you stay competitive.

Too many businesses have spent a ton of money on their website just to let them sit and do nothing for them. It's time to change that by structuring your website based on these four elements. It will turn your website into a powerful and useful asset for your business that works for you. Now let's move forward to Pillar #2 on Mobile.

PILLAR #2: MOBILE

Welcome to Pillar #2 Mobile. The recent Mobile Movement has quickly changed the dynamic of marketing as you know it.

Mobile now has become the leading way today's consumers receive and engage with information. Indeed, the mobile revolution is helping to lead the shift from the Information Age transforming into the Connected Age.

Mobile, when used for marketing, can operate as the center piece for most marketing strategies; becoming an integrated hub to any solid online or offline marketing campaign.

The growing power of mobile is showing to be just as effective as TV and the Internet. Recent evidence continues to surface, revealing the reach ability of mobile. A recent quote released from The **New York Times™** stated:

"Mobile is the most powerful advertising medium ever invented".

Now you may be asking yourself "ever invented"? Really? This huge claim grows legs when you stop to think about ALL the things we DO with our Smart Phones.

Mobile Uses: (things like):

1. Making Calls
2. Text Messages
3. Receive Emails
4. Watching Videos
5. Social Media

These are just a few activities mobile is used for. The biggest shocker of all is how we never leave home (*work /school*) without our mobile devices.

It's like they have become physically a part of us. Seriously, ask yourself these **4 Questions**. So you can personally realize the Power of Mobile.

How Important Is Your Mobile Really:

1. How often do you look at your mobile phone?
2. How far do you let your phone physically get from you?
3. How many of your text messages do you read?
4. How fast do you read new text messages?

The point of answering these questions is to open your eyes to your **OWN** mobile behavior patterns. The fact is if YOU do this, so does your "Ideal Customer".

Next I'm going to remove the 500 pound elephant in the room, by explaining exactly what this mean for your business? Here are a few ways to use Mobile to reach customers "*Where They Are*" while creating a great user experience.

Mobile Websites: The first element we're going to look at is "*Mobile Websites*".

Having a Mobile Website is very different from your standard Desktop Website. This Website is designed especially for Mobile devices.

The importance behind this is HUGE since more and more people are accessing the Internet via Mobile phones than Desktops nowadays.

It's imperative your Business Website has both a Desktop and Mobile Friendly Version. Remember the training from "*Understanding Your Market*".

Where the search data showed how many people are looking for you via Mobile Devices. Now let's really think about this for a moment.

If your "*Ideal Customers*" are Mobile shouldn't your business be? This little tweak alone can add 10 to 40% to your bottom line. It has become a must-have for all small businesses.

SMS Text Messages: The second element we're going to examine is "*Text Messaging*".

Text Messaging has now become the new norm of communication. On a daily basis there are over 2 Billion searches in Google™ and over 4 Billion Text Messages are sent. Can you see **WHY** Text Messaging has become so popular.

The good news for businesses is Text Messages have an average Open Rate of 95% and 88% of those recipients take **ACTION** the same day! How's that for instant results.

Text Messages are a Great Way to:

1. Keep in Touch with Customers
2. Sending out Promotional Offers
3. Sharing useful Content with Customers
4. Send out Appointment Reminders

Mobile Landing Pages: Next, the third element in Mobile is called "*Mobile Landing Pages*". Similar to a Lead Capture Page for your Desktop Website. Mobile Landing Pages are used in a very similar fashion, but are mobile friendly. These types of pages quickly draw mobile users to take action.

Some uses for Mobile Landing Pages include:

Building a List, Promoting Special Offers or Events, Generating New Fans via Social Media Landing Pages; the best part about **ALL** of these elements is their ability to work together creating an explosive mobile experience.

QR Codes: The last element in this Mobile Pillar is "*QR Codes*". If you don't already know what a QR Code is, it's simply a quick response code designed for mobile phones.

This barcode quickly allows a mobile user to scan an image and be directed to any destination which creates an interactive and engaging experience for the mobile user.

For instance you could use a QR Code to:

1. Send People to Your Website (*read blog post*)
2. Send People to Your Fan Page (*any network*)
3. Send People a Text Message (*coupon, etc.*)
4. Send People to Virtual Video (*tour, test drive, welcome or promotional videos*)

There are unlimited things you could do with QR Codes. Just use your creativity and let it run free.

Recap:

Okay, let's quickly recap what you learned about Mobile in *Pillar 2*.

Mobile Websites:

First you learned how important it is to have both a Desktop and Mobile Version of your website. This has become the **KEY** to Never missing an opportunity for new business.

SMS Messages:

Next you learned how text messages are the most effective way to reach customers. Allowing you to reach customers On-The-Go and in Real Time.

Mobile Landing Pages: Then you learned how Mobile Landing Pages are very similar to website capture pages, but designed especially for mobile users. This is a powerful tool for building a list.

QR Codes:

Last, you learned how QR Codes quickly connect customers with anything you want- making it fun and easy to get additional information.

Homework:

Your homework from this module is to examine your current marketing plan and see if you have these *4 Elements* actively in place. Then decide are you using them correctly. If not it's time to start making adjustments.

Remember Mobile is not going anywhere. Mobile is not a fad. Mobile is not the future. Mobile is **NOW**! The sooner you get on board and start injecting mobile into your business, the sooner you'll start becoming "**Relevant**" to the Modern Consumer. You did a great job for making it through this module. Up next is Pillar #3 Social Media.

PILLAR #3: SOCIAL MEDIA

Welcome to Pillar #3 Social Media. Unless lately you've been living under a rock, by now you have heard of Social Media. This new age phenomenon has forever changed the way individuals go about communicating online. From friends with friends to brands with consumers- everyone, no matter how big or small, is encouraged to use their **"VOICE"** socially. Social Media has become to consumers the *new word of mouth*- a faster way to find and share information. Never before could someone post what they think or feel and it be seen by millions.

Placing this type of social power into consumer hands has deeply impacted our business economy. How? By transforming marketing from a one-sided conversation into a *Reputation Economy*.

Opening the doors to a two way conversation, the recent popularity of sites like:

1. Facebook™
2. Twitter™
3. LinkedIn™
4. Google Plus™
5. Pinterest™
6. YouTube™ (*to name a few*)

Have greatly influenced a **HUGE** part on how modern consumers perform research and engage with businesses. It's important that your company has a Social Media plan in place.

A plan that intensely focuses on *"Relationship Building"* and not just marketing; building strong relationships are key.

The more people who can relate with your brands identity, the better. Every small business must understand how important this is. Remember the **"Buying Process"** and how the first step inside that process is research.

Recent studies show *"72% of consumers currently buy products and services based simply on a recommendation from a friend or online review"*.

Social Media directly positions your company face to face with consumers. The main problem many businesses have with social media isn't setting up accounts on these networks.

It is understanding how to use these networks effectively; really sparking the **GROWTH** of their social presence and engaging with their targeted audience; bonding enough to *"Turn Fans into Customers"*.

Here are a few ways to use Social Media to interact, engage, and grow your social audience.

Scheduled Posts: The first element we're going to look at is *"Scheduled Posts"*. It's extremely important when building relationships socially the conversation **NEVER** stops. The conversation with your audience must always be constant. To accomplish this you can create "*Scheduled Posts*" that talk about your business and provide quality useful information.

The better your content, the more responsive and engaged fans will be. Now I know you're busy and pressed for time constantly to be updating your social networks. That's why I suggest pre-scheduling your posts daily or even weeks at a time.

There are many social tools to help you do this. But a great way to manage your Social Networks is a tool called *Hootsuite*™. Simply use the free version of this tool to help pre-schedule your messages in advance. Also link together all your social networks inside the program. It's really simple and easy to do. When setting up your messages be sure to pre-schedule 3-5 "*Update*" posts daily. Remember to use images, videos and questions to engage fans.

Grab a pen and write this formula down. When your scheduling post updates always keep your conversations 70% Educational or Entertaining and 30% Sales Messages. I've found this recipe works best for keeping fans attention.

The key here is to focus on building relationships. Real relationships that increase sales because your audience **Know You, Like You, and Trust You**. This is super important when it applies to sales.

<u>Images:</u> The second element we're going to look at is "*Images*".

Using images in your post updates is extremely powerful. One of the fastest ways to go viral and receive a flood of new fans is images. But the secret ingredient that makes images catchy and stand out more are "***Captions***". We've all seen this before. You're online and come across some type of image with a funny or interesting tagline.

What's the first thing you do when you see something like this? You shared it with friends, right? Especially if it made you laugh or looked cool. Works like gang busters every time.

This is probably why Facebook™ recently paid one billion to acquire Instagram™- also why sites like Pinterest™ receive over 1 million visitors a month.

So what does the future of Social Media look like to you? Image friendly baby? Here are a couple tips to remember when using images.

Make sure your images:

1. Are Funny or Catchy Visually
2. Relate to Your Business (*product or service*)
3. Possess a Call-To-Action

When it comes to a **Call-To-Action**, you want to say things like:

> *"Click to Share with Your Friends"*
> *"Click Share so Your Friends can see this"*
> *"Click Like to give this a Thumbs Up"*

Encourage people to engage with your content. Don't abuse this tactic but blend it in with other quality content such as videos and blog posts.

Post Special Offers: The third element in this module is "*Posting Special Offers*".

This is where the magic happens. Special offers to consumers are like honey to bees. Both rich and sweet because everyone loves a bargain jam packed with value.

Presenting the right offer at the right time can encourage current fans and draw new ones to take action. Really get involved with what's happening at your business.

An effective and easy way to do this is directly on your Facebook page or any other social network. Remember to:

1. Host Events
2. Advertise Special Contests
3. Giveaways (*like vouchers, trials, coupons, etc.*)

Allow people to claim their prize "instantly" by performing some type of **ACTION** (*make a call, text to, scan this, etc.*).

This is perfect for attracting Likes, Tweets, and Plus +1's; really spreading word of mouth about your business. So review your "*Customer Avatar*" and "*Competition Audit Reports*".

Identify what others are doing in your market. What type of special offers are people responding to? Then get creative. Plan out at least 2-3 Special Offers or Contests you could do monthly.

Remember all these offers you create can be cross promoted on all the other marketing pillars. Make sure everything you do points to a single "**Sales Funnel**" while simultaneously building a *5 STAR Reputation*.

Promote Your Social Channels:

The last element inside our Social Media Pillar is "*Promoting Your Social Channels*".

The perfect way to get attention to your social networks and attract non-fans is promoting them everywhere. First choose which networks matter the most for your business presence or ones you're most comfortable with. For majority of people this will consist mainly of Facebook™, Twitter™ and YouTube™.

Next you want to place your Facebook™ and Twitter™ URL links on everything you do- just like you would do with your Website URL. Here are some key places to build social integration:

1. Add Your Social Links to All (*articles, videos*)
2. Add Your Social Links to All Print Ads
3. All Forms of Communication (*anything consumers see)*

Recap:

Let's recap about what we've learned in *Pillar 3* on Social Media.

Schedule Posts:
First you learned how important when building relationships, the conversation with your audience remains constant. Allowing consumers access to the personality behind the brand. Scheduling posts is how to accomplish this.

Images: Next you learned in detail how images are extremely powerful and one of the best ways to engage fans. Relationships are everything.

Posting Special Offers: Then you learned how posting special offers and contests spread like wildfire- a simple but effective viral method.

Promoting Social Channels: Last you learned how proper social integration will naturally grow and promote your social networks. This builds the Know, Like, and Trust factors.

Homework:

Your homework from this module is to examine your current Social Media Marketing Plan. If you don't have one, it's time to start. Then see if you have these *4 Elements* in place.

Next decide are you using them correctly. If not it's time to start making small adjustments. Social Media is huge with sites like Facebook™ having over 1 Billion active users.

You know for a fact that your "**Ideal Customer**" uses Social Media. So "*Join the Conversation*" and start reaching customers where they are- learning how to convert leads into fans and fans into customers. Hopefully you're super excited about what you've learned thus far. I know I am just from sharing it. I'll see you in the next Pillar on Email.

PILLAR # 4: EMAIL

Welcome back everyone to Pillar # 4 Email. During this module you're going to learn how to use Email to effectively engage and communicate with customers.

Email Marketing used correctly will help build relationships that improve your bottom-line while helping spread the social "*Shareability*" of your company's content. We are going to revolutionize the standard usage of Email in this training.

This is very similar to Social Media. People send emails when they want to share links, videos or images with friends and family. Statistics show 78% of people share content via Email, compared to 22% shared on Social Media.

So what exactly does this all mean for your business? Simply that Email Marketing used for your business **WORKS** and is highly effective. But I have a surprise for you.

Take a guess about the "*Secret Sauce*" that's going to add steroids to your Email Marketing Campaigns. **VIDEO**!

We're going to add Video to spice up your Email Campaigns. Why video? Because choosing to combine Videos power with Email delivers your personality and message to the inbox.

Adding Video allows customers to interact with your content, more than text and images alone.
Here are a few ways to use Video Emails to build relationships.

Developing a large **"Customer Database"** to send through your unique Sales Funnel becomes easy with video; turning new prospects into fans and fans into customers.

<u>**Your Website:**</u> The first element inside our Email Pillar is *"Your Website"*.

Remember Pillar #1 on **"Your Website"**, where we discussed Lead Capturing and how Landing Pages help add subscribers.

It's really important to make sure you have "Sign Up" opportunities throughout your website. So when visitors are browsing your website to learn more information about your Company's products or services, they can easily recognize the *Value* in Joining your List.

There are two ways that I recommend setting up Video Emails:

BombBomb: My first recommendation is using a company called BombBomb™. They are an amazing Video Email platform and do everything we talked about plus more. I personally use this platform for my business.

(Or you can try)

Aweber: My second recommendation is using a company called an Aweber™. They are an Email Marketing platform and also create Optin forms. But combining this with Video you must use YouTube™.

Just insert a screenshot of the video and link in the Email body itself. Direct interested customers to a *YouTube™ Channel*, *Blog Post*, or *Landing Page*. Either way you're comfortable, both are easy and effective.

<u>Your Facebook Page:</u> The second element we're going to look at is your "*Facebook™ Page*".

In our step by step process of creating a "***Custom Sales Funnel***", you're going to add a Landing Page inside your Facebook™ account. Sounds pretty cool huh? Here's how you do this. On your company Fan Page you will have to add a "**Tab**" button. Next you want to name the tab something catchy, so people would want to check it out.

When someone visits that page, make sure to have some type of High-Value Offer to encourage visitors to subscribe. The Headline on your page should read something like:

"Subscribe to our Newsletter (*or VIP List*) to receive Exclusive Updates and an INSTANT Coupon for 25% off your Next Visit".

Remember to offer something *FREE* with high perceived value. You get the idea- this is very powerful stuff.

<u>Physical Capture:</u> The second element you're going to examine is called "*Physical Capture*". Now this strategy depends on the type of business you operate. But, if your Business already:

1. Talks with Customers (*Over the Phone*)
2. Meets with Customers face-to-face (*Consultative or Transactional*)

The next time you're talking with or in front of a customer, during the transaction or end of conversation "*ask*" for their contact information.

Either collect an Email or have them Scan a QR Code that's leads to Mobile Capture page. I know this sounds simple but it is super effective. It's

NOT always what you know, but what you do! Train your employees to do the exact same for all phone and service calls. If you're in retail or some very similar type industry, the greatest opportunity to perform this is at the "**Point of Sale**". Even if they haven't bought from you yet, they're interested and you have their attention.

Learn to recognize these opportunities inside your company's daily operations. Then make sure to direct those interested consumers to a dedicated "**Special Offer**" (*via Desktop or Mobile Landing Page*) and enter them into your Sales Funnel.

Recap:

Let's recap what you have learned in *Pillar 4* on Email.

Your Website:
First you learned how having various "Sign-Up" opportunities throughout your Website increases Optin Conversions.

Your Facebook Page:
Next you learned how to add an Email Optin page inside your Facebook page. Then present a High-Value Offer to increase our Optin Conversions.

Physical Capture:
Last you learned how important it is collecting customer information, making the most from any type of customer contact- always pushing every interested prospect into your Sales Funnel.

Homework:

Your homework from this module is to examine your Current Marketing plan. Take a look at these *3 Elements* and make sure you have everything in place, then decide if you're using them correctly. If not, it's time to start making adjustments.

Hopefully you can see how Video Email drives such a high level of consumer engagement while consistently increasing your Brands Relationships and ROI.

Congratulations! You made it through another module. You should feel great. You're moving right along learning and brainstorming new ideas. Remember to take notes and pace yourself. See you in the next Pillar on Video.

PILLAR # 5: VIDEO

Hello again, welcome to Pillar # 5 Video. Video is very Powerful and Personal. In this module you're going to learn how to use Video to enhance your Campaigns Voice, Create Social Content and Generate a Buzz around your business.

This untapped love people have for television has transferred over to online video. If you thought watching television was huge news, these online video stats should greatly open your eyes to the influential power of Video.

We all know how **BIG** the Internet is. But did you know in 2013 around 80% of all Internet traffic will be "Video".

This is fantastic news for businesses; especially since 48% of people who see a Video Ad take some form of positive action. Additional case studies show video can bring:

1. 55% Visitor Increase to a Company Website
2. 30% Physical In-Store Increase
3. Increase Incidence of NEW purchases by 24%

Really trying to understand video a little better, you notice how Video whether on TV or Online is all about the story and audience.

What Does this Mean for Your Business?

Simply that Online Video, if used correctly, will increase:

1. Brand Awareness
2. Drive Online Engagement
3. Create Viewer Action

Taking advantage of this power will lead to more inquires and sales. Let's check out a few ways that Video can grow your audience and create a social microphone for your business.

Targeted Videos: The first element inside our Video Pillar is "*Targeted Videos*".

Remember the module on "***Understanding Your Market***" where you discovered Questions and Topics that your market wanted to know about?

This is where that information comes in handy. Review each keyword (*search phrase*) that made your list. Next you want to create a video for each term.

The types of Videos you can make are:

1. Personal Videos (*where people see you*)
2. Screencast Videos (*using PowerPoint*)

In these Videos make sure to cover things like *General Questions*, *Industry Questions*, *Fears*, *How- To's* and *Problems;* providing real solutions to customers and positioning your business as the market's top company. Just don't say you're the **BEST**, show them you are.

Inside these videos you should cover "***Topic Promotions***", based on the needs of the customer. Create ultra-targeted promotional messages that identify with your ideal customers.

Messages that when heard by consumers create a "*That's Me*" experience; the beauty of this is once you have created these videos you can syndicate them everywhere, including places like:

Your Blog: Where they can be used for creating more quality content that customers want and need.

Social Networks: Try mixing them in with your scheduled posts. Drive customers back to your website or wherever else you want traffic with Special Offers, Promotions, etc.

Emails: Remember you just learned about the power of Video Email. You can use these videos for newsletter updates or adding people to your subscriber list.

Social Mobile Landing Pages: When we talked about Mobile you learned how you could create video landing pages.

In-Store Promotions: If you run any in-store promotional videos, these are great to have playing as foot traffic comes in and out. Just use your imagination and have fun with it!

Video Testimonials: The second element you're going to look at is "*Video Testimonials*". This strategy creates an instant bond of trust between you and your potential customers. It's absolutely unbelievable how powerful this is.

Every company believes they are the best. What better way to show you are to customers, then with Video. When it comes to sales, people buy from people they:

1. Know
2. Like
3. Trust

Using Video this way satisfies all three in one single swoop. At the end of the day, people buy from people. So remember to ask all new or previous satisfied customers if they're willing to make a quick video, showing how much they like your business or why they do business with you.

This is like looking at a box of cake mix with the picture of a cake on it. What exactly sells the mix? The picture of finished cake, right? Well, symbolically this is the same. Prospects can see the end results of buying your products or services upfront directly from their peers.

This method is very cheap and cost effective to do. Grab your iPhone or flip camera and make your own videos. Also take pictures of happy customers that do business with you, then post them online. Show how happy customers are when they buy your products or services.

Recap:

Okay let's recap on what you learned in *Pillar 5* on Video.

Targeted Videos:
First you learned about how targeted videos can really engage customers and encourage them to take action. We also discussed how you can syndicate these videos everywhere for ultimate exposure.

Video Testimonials:
Then you learned how video testimonials can create an unbelievable bond with customers. Helping customers establish the Know, Like and Trust factors- which is why people buy in the first place.

Homework:

Your homework in this module is to examine your current marketing plan and see if these *2 Elements* are in place. If not, take a close look at possible ways you can implement video into your business.

The amount of Social Proof and Brand Awareness videos can produce for your business is limitless.

I hope you're on fire, seeing how powerful video can be for business. It's a great communication tool.

I'm very proud of you for making it through this module. We have one more Pillar left called Offline. I'll see you in the next module.

PILLAR #6: OFFLINE

Welcome to the final Pillar #6 Offline. This is one of my personal favorite Pillars. Depending on your company's business model, some of the strategies you're going to learn can be applied to online as well.

The beauty about this pillar is how it leverages the power of all the other pillar strategies, really expanding the various ways to reach your Ideal Customer.

At this stage you're going to utilize all the communication channels that your modern consumer currently uses. Positing your business this way, makes you instantly visible and relevant to their daily activities.

This strategic move reveals the Internet's social evolution to gradually merge the Off-line and Online worlds together. Step back and think about *ALL* the recent merging of modern technology lately. Americans can easily access every kind of information while on the go.

Our Mobile devices such as Smartphones and Tablets have become a **"Central Hub"** for just about everything now days. Keeping us connected 24/7, while providing us access to: *The Internet, Social media, Video, Emails and Text Messages*.

This is game changing news for all businesses, allowing you a better way to create super targeted <u>Inbound</u> and <u>Outbound</u> Marketing messages for your audience. Truly sparking consumers' interest in such a way that will drive "*Off-line Consumers Online*" and "*Online Consumers Off-line*"; making the communication circle go full swing leaving no major channel unturned.

Sounds crazy I know, but take the time to look at each Pillar individually. Then think how **YOU** access the:

1. Internet
2. Social Media
3. Video
4. Emails
5. Text Messages

Look at your own behaviors and realize if you're doing this so are your customers. Here are a few strategies to help grow your business Offline that will draw Engaged Prospects and Encourage them to buy your products or services. Let's get started.

<u>Customer Re-Activator</u>: The first element inside this pillar we're going to take a look at, I call "*Customer Re-Activator*".

One of the fastest ways to bring in NEW Business and Generate NEW Revenue is to reactivate past customers. Studies show it costs 5x's more to get a **NEW** Client, than Reactivating a previous one!

It's so important that you learn this. The very 1st Step you want to take is "*Data Mining*". Start looking over all your existing or past transactions with customers or maybe go over any:

1. Old Customer Profiles
2. Old Applications
3. Old Lists

Anything really that has an Email, or maybe a Mobile phone number. So you can compile them into one master customer database (list). Really try to dig deep here.

Next after you have compiled your list of present or past customers, you must create a reason for contacting them. Some type of "*Irresistible Offer*" that would present huge value in the eyes of your customer. Things like:

1. Free Gift
2. Gas Card
3. Credit Voucher
4. In-Store Credit
5. Coupon

Anything of High Perceived Value. This builds positive word-of-mouth and also helps generates positive reviews putting the *Law of Reciprocity* in action. Plus customers love to feel appreciated. Simply remind them, they are!

The *2nd Step* is making sure when you start your message campaign via Email or Mobile (maybe both) that you create a benefit driven Subject Line or Headline.

Remember customers are thinking "*what's in it for me*"? So appeal to that. Doing this will do wonders for your open rates.

The *3rd and final Step* is making sure your messages have a "**Call-To-Action**". Links inside of your messages such as "*Click Here for Benefit XYZ*", give them a reason to click, to engage.

Most importantly, make sure the links inside your messages go to some type of Lead Capture or Mobile Landing Page, so that you can build a list of "interested" targeted buyers.

These are **NOT** traditional leads because they already have bought from you in the past. That makes them a hundred times more valuable.

New Customer Oasis: The second element inside Pillar 6 Offline is what I call "*New Customer Oasis*".

One of the most effective ways to get people in the door is Direct Mail. Yes, direct mail still works ladies and gents. Many businesses today still are seeing great returns with direct mail. Especially if you step it up with a modern twist. Try using bright colorful and large catchy UV coated designed postcards.

The trick and secret sauce to making this work is:

1. Focusing on Local Consumers (*within a 5 Mile Radius*)
2. Have Special Offer / Promotion (*Benefit Driven Headline*)
3. Having a Call-To-Action (*Text Keyword to Number or Scan QR Code to Receive Coupon Instantly*).

This will help spread the word-of-mouth about your companies' promotions and help produce a positive buzz. Check your local post office for special programs for cheap postcards mailings. Simple but effective, just try it and see.

Reoccurring Income Delight: The last element in Pillar 6 is what I call "*Reoccurring Income Delight*".

Sounds delicious, right? Imagine being able to discover *NEW* income streams and implement them into your Business. Would that make you happy? Well, now you can. Just analyze your business and find something that you could offer consumers on a monthly basis. Steps to discover Reoccurring Income are:

1. Thinking of what Products or Services you Sell the Most of?
2. How Often do you Sell that Item Monthly?
3. How could these Products or Services be Bundled for Savings?

The idea here is to think membership. Where a customer could save a certain percentage off all the same Products or Services they already use. Pretty awesome, huh?

All you have to do is determine your "*Current Customer Value*" (if you don't how to do that use our **Visionary Concepts ROI Calculator** in the resource section) and then use that same customer information to determine a fair membership price to charge customers.

Recap:

Okay let's recap what you learned inside *Pillar 6 Offline*.

Customer Re-Activator:

First you learned how reactivating previous customers is five times cheaper than acquiring new customers. This is a great way to save money on current monthly advertising.

New Customer Oasis:

Next you learned how using direct-mail with mobile call to actions drives foot traffic and can build a list of interested prospects fast- extremely interactive and effective.

Reoccurring Income Delight:

Last you learned how to create a new income stream for your business. This strategy provides guaranteed revenue you can count on every month without any need for further advertising or sales.

Homework:

Your homework from this module is to examine your current marketing plan. Identify if these *3 Elements* exist inside your current marketing process. If not, then you need to start making adjustments.

Alright, hopefully your brain is flooding with new ways on how to start implementing these tactics into your business. I am so proud of you for making it this far, it shows that you're really committed to making a difference in your business and **you will**.

Get ready to learn how to bring all of what you learn together and create an action plan designed for success, that's recession proof.

Notes

BRINGING IT TOGETHER

Welcome to "*Bringing It Together*". This is where the magic happens. During this module you're going to learn how to form everything you've learned in the "Understanding Your Market" and Pillar Training into a Winning Recession-Proof Marketing Blueprint.

The point of this whole course is teaching small businesses how to create their own custom "**Sales Funnel**" that maximizes conversions. Improving conversion rates is the fastest way to increase profits and who doesn't need more revenue in their business? All of us do.

Businesses must focus on setting up marketing systems that work for them 24 hours a day, 365 days a year without fail. What are the three major things every business desperately wants? **More Customers, More Revenue** and **More Profits**!

Improving conversion rates is the fastest way to accomplish that goal. But before you can work on Converting Prospects into Customers, you must first Capture Them. You must Capture to Convert. Remember that 99% of interested prospects that visit a business leave and never returns.

This is why you worked extremely **HARD** to "Understand Our Market" in the beginning and

Optimize your 6 Pillars. When it comes to sales people buy when they are ready to buy, **NOT** when you're ready to sale- waiting until they actually see themselves in the Product or Service. The shocking statistic is how "*81% of Sales require 5 Touches*" (*or contact*) and "*10% of Sales required 4 Touches*". But sadly, only "*10%* of Companies actually make 5 Touches- which means most businesses are simply giving up too soon or quitting right before consumers decide to buy.

You can clearly understand the science behind why sales take multiple of touches (*contacts*); Especially when you look at how the Buying Process works in detail. Each stage has a different action, which requires a unique response in your Sales Funnel.

BUYING PROCESS

Realize Problem or Need	Perform Research	Establish Buying Criteria	Purchase
Stage I	Stage II	Stage III	Stage VI

During the First Stage a Customer realizes he or she has a *Problem*, *Want* or *Need* and searches for a Solution. Moving forward to the Second Stage, a Customer begins to *Research* and *Understand* any possible solutions they have available.

Pushing along to the Third Stage, a customer decides what company offers the *Best Price* and *Quality*. This stage positions the customer to *Buy* during the Fourth Stage. All that's left is presenting your *Irresistible Offer* (*Trial, Discount or Coupon*).

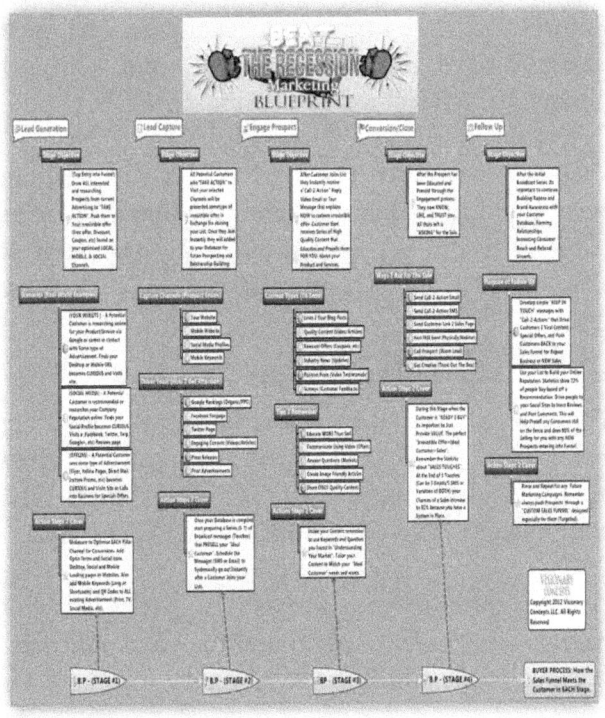

Now take a close look at my **Beat the Recession Blueprint** above. This blueprint is designed to meet the Customer at <u>Each Stage</u> in the "**Buying Process**", systematically making it really easy for consumers to be engaged where they are. My *Beat the Recession Marketing Blueprint* consists of 5 Key Sections:

1. Lead Generation
2. Lead Capture
3. Engagement
4. Close/Conversion
5. Follow Up

Before you start diving into each section, make sure you have already set up and optimized each Pillar for Conversions.

This step is extremely vital to get the absolute best ROI from each marketing channel. The first section inside our Blueprint that you want to examine in detail is *"Lead Generation"*.

LEAD GENERATION:

This Stage in our process is what you call *"Top Entry"* into the Sales Funnel. Here you will draw interested and researching prospects from ALL your current advertising to **"TAKE ACTION"**.

Pushing them to your irresistible offer (*discount, coupon, free offer, etc.*) found on your optimized Local, Mobile and Social Channels.

Let's take a deeper look at some real world scenarios; realistic examples of how exactly this stage would happen.

1. **Your Website:** A potential customer is researching online for information about your products and services via Google™, or comes in contact with some type of flyer advertisement. They locate your company's Desktop or Mobile URL, become *CURIOUS* and visit site.

2. **Social Media:** A potential customer is personally recommended or researches your business Reputation online. They find your company's online Social Profile and become *CURIOUS*. Then he or she visits a (Facebook™, Twitter™, Yelp™, Google Plus™, etc.) Company Review page.

3. **Offline:** A potential customer comes in contact with some form of your company's Advertisement (Flyer, Yellow Pages™, Direct Mail, In-store Promo, etc.); becomes *CURIOUS* and either visits a website or call your business for special offers.

Action Steps to Cover:

Make sure to Optimize *EACH* Pillar marketing channel for Conversions. Add Optin Forms and Social icons everywhere possible, including all Desktop, Social and Mobile Landing Pages. Also add Mobile Keywords (*Long or Short-codes*) and QR Codes to all existing Advertisements (*Print, TV, Social Media, etc.*).

The second section inside our Blueprint is "*Lead Capture*".

LEAD CAPTURE:

The Stage objective here is reaching all potential customers who initially "**TOOK ACTION**".

Those who visited your selected Channels will be presented some type of irresistible offer in exchange for Joining your List. Once a consumer joins, **_Instantly_** they're added to your Database for future Prospecting and Relationship Building.

Let's take a look at the Capture Channels that a prospect would enter. These are Channels your consumer has *EASY* access too.

1. Your Website
2. Your Social Media Profiles
3. Your Mobile Website
4. Mobile Keywords You Create

Here are some of the most powerful and effective "**_Driver Tools_**" that will help you get consumers attention.

1. Search Engine Rankings (*Organic & PPC*)
2. Building an Online 5 Star Reputation
3. Facebook Fan page™
4. Twitter™ Page
5. Engaging Content (*Videos & Articles*)
6. Press Releases
7. Print Advertisements

Action Steps to Cover:

Once your Database is compiled, start preparing a Series of 5 to 7 Broadcast Messages (*Touches*) that *PRESELL* your **"Ideal Customer"**. Schedule the Messages (*SMS or Email*) to systematically go out Instantly, after a Customer Joins your List.

The third section inside our Blueprint is "*Engage Prospect*".

ENGAGE PROSPECT:

The Stage objective here is after a Customer Joins your List. They will instantly receive a "*Call-2-Action*" reply via *Video Email* or *Text Message*. That message quickly explains *HOW* to redeem your company's irresistible offer. A Customer then receives a Series of High-Quality Content that *Educates* and *Presells* them automatically **FOR YOU**- informing them about your Products and Services.

Let's take a look at the types of engaging content to send during this stage. These are proven to work the best.

1. Links to Your Blog Post
2. Quality Content (*Videos & Articles*)
3. Relevant Offers (*Coupons, etc.*)
4. Industry News (*Updates*)
5. Positive Press (*Video Testimonials*)
6. Surveys (*Customer Feedback*)

Here are some great tips and general guide lines to remember when sending out engaging content.

1. Educate **MORE** Than Sell
2. Communicate Using Video (*Often*)
3. Answer Questions (*Market*)
4. Create Image Friendly Articles
5. Share **ONLY** Quality Content

Action Steps to Cover:

Inside your content remember to use Keywords and Questions you found in "***Understanding Your Market***" phase. Tailor your Content to match your "**Ideal Customers**" needs and wants.

The fourth section inside our Blueprint is the "*Conversion*".

CONVERSION:

The Stage objective here is after the Prospect has been properly educated and thoroughly warmed up during the Engagement process- they now *Know*, *Like* and *Trust* you. They are now ready to **BUY**, so all that's left is "**ASKING**" for the sale.

Let's take a look at ways to ask for the sale. Don't over think this. Everything from here *FOWARD* is fun and simple because the relationship with the prospect has already been established.

Ask for the sale by:

1. Sending Out Call-2-Action Emails
2. Sending Out Call-2-Action Text Messages
3. Sending Customers a Link to Your Sales Page
4. Hosting **FREE** Events (*Physically or Webinar*)
5. Calling Prospects (*Warm Leads*)
6. Getting Creative (*Think Out the Box*)

Actions Steps to Cover:

During this Stage when the Customer is "**Ready 2 Buy**" it's important to just Provide *VALUE*. The perfect "**Irresistible Offer + Ideal Customer = Sales**". Remember the Statistic from earlier about "*SALES TOUCHES*".

At the end of 5 Touches (*can be 5 Emails / 5 SMS or Variation of BOTH*). Your chances of a sale increase to 81% all because you have a strong sales process in place working for you.

The fifth and final section inside our Blueprint is "*Follow-Up*".

FOLLOW-UP:

This Stage objective happens after a consumer receives their initial *Broadcast Series Messages*. The focus here is to continue building rapport and brand awareness with your Customer Database.

Forming relationships, increasing customer reach and expanding referral growth- let's look at some ways you can implement follow up into our sales process.

1. Developing simple "**KEEP IN TOUCH**" messages (*email or text*) with "**Call-2-Actions**" that drive customers to Viral Content, Special Offers and Push Customers *BACK* to your Sales Funnel for repeat business or new sales

2. Using your Customer List to Build an "**Online Reputation**". Statistics show 72% of people buy based on a recommendation. Drive people to your Social Sites to leave reviews and post comments.

This will help presell any consumers still on the fence. Creating "**Social Proof**" does 90% of the hard selling for you without any new prospects entering into the funnel.

Action Steps to Cover:

All you have to do is "***Rinse and Repeat***" this for any future marketing campaigns. Remember, always push prospects through a "**Custom Sales Funnel**" designed especially for them (*Targeted*).

Now you can see from day one, to the point of sale how you're going to *Capture New Leads* and *Engage Prospects* through a custom designed "**Sales Funnel**" made especially for your Ideal Customer.

When everything is set up and in place, your Custom Sales Funnel will look something like the image above.

This is a workable system where you can add or take away. The point here is creating a system that: *Generates Leads*, Captures *Leads*, *Converts Leads into Sales* and *Follows Up* like clockwork. Now your business has such a system.

The majority of this course is spent on Setting Up and Optimizing your channels. Laying the foundation, making sure you understand **WHY** to do this or the psychology and science behind your actions. Most people want a magic pill, but I've just given you **PURE** muscle. Apply that muscle and build your business.

Congratulations. You are now ready for action. You made it! Be proud of yourself. Most people don't make it this far. This shows you want to be successful and are willing to put in the **WORK** to get there.

Nothing comes easy in life, and if it did, you wouldn't appreciate it. Take this system and make it your own. Use the keys inside this book to go out there and *Beat The Recession.*

One of the most important principles about marketing to remember is: understanding your customer and speaking their language. They're waiting to do business with such a company.

The Recession has presented many hurdles, but it also has presented opportunity- an opportunity for those who will rise up and dare to be different; learning to fight back by doing something **NEW**.

Audit your Company's current Marketing Plan and Sales Process in detail. Locate the areas of improvement and fix them. Don't go back into the same arena you just lost in and repeat the same old marketing mistakes. **Albert Einstein said the definition of Insanity is:**

"Doing the same thing over and over again-expecting different results."

You've come this far and now you're ready for action!

If you need any assistance or would like a *FREE (Done for You)* **Marketing Profitability Audit**-please don't hesitate to contact me through our Beat The Recession Marketing website.

Make sure to check out the next module on what kind of "**Results to Expect**" from putting this marketing system in place. Also, remember to download the "**Beat the Recession Blueprint PDF**; then watch my FREE Bonus Videos on **What's My Reputation** & **Why 2 Go Mobile** located in the resource section.

Thank you for reading my book. It has been my pleasure sharing the keys to the Kingdom with you. Make a difference in your business and apply your new mindset and knowledge. I hope you received an extreme amount of value from this course.

Notes

_____

_____

_____

_____

_____

_____

_____

_____

_____

_____

_____

_____

_____

_____

_____

_____

_____

_____

_____

_____

_____

_____

RESULTS TO EXPECT

Before you leave this course and jump into action, I would like to share with you the type of results you can expect from implementing a *Beat The Recession Marketing* campaign.

These results depend greatly on many factors; from your offer type, competition strength, your work ethic and a list of other things. So the results I'm going to share are realistic for any business that works hard and really apply itself.

Once you see how our *Visionary ROI Calculator* work, you will clearly understand how realistic a plan for receiving Marketing ROI could be. There are *5 Elements* that our calculator is designed for. We are going to focus only on *3 Elements*.

1. Sales Booster Formula
2. Advanced ROI Formula
3. Customer Value Formula

The points of these formulas are to help motivate you by showing you results in advance. I know how it feels to think you're wasting time and money. Here's a little way to logically remove that fear by replacing it with solid numbers (*data*).

Most business orientated professionals are very analytical. So let's get started breaking each of these formulas down. The first formula we're going to learn is called "Sales Booster".

SALES BOOSTER:

The Visionary *Sales Booster Formula* is designed to examine the profitability metrics inside your business. Then to visually show you how a few incremental changes inside certain metrics can do wonders for your businesses bottom-line.

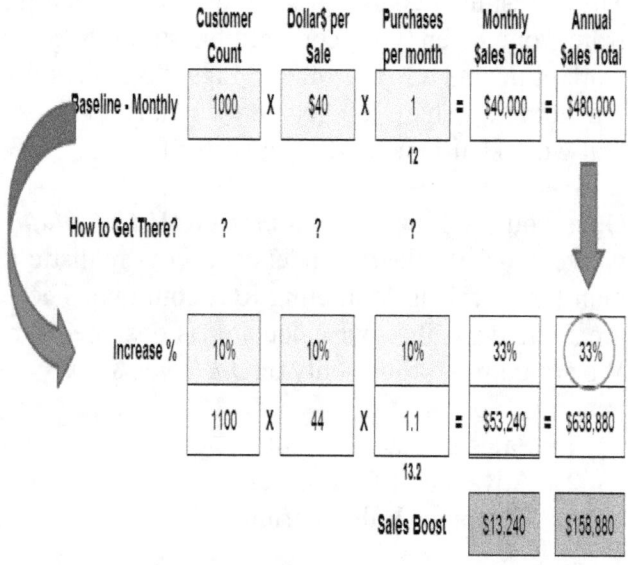

Let's say for example that I'm a local restaurant owner in San Diego, California. My restaurant receives 1000 customers on a monthly basis. Each of my customers normally spends $40 on dinner for two. Customers usually visit my place of business one time a month.

In this example, the restaurant would generate $40,000 in sales monthly and $480,000 annually.

These are basic profit and loss numbers that every business owner today clearly understands. This leaves you with one question: What does this mean for my bottom-line?

The answer to the million dollar question is revealed by focusing solely on 3 Major Metrics. Your **Customer Count**, **Dollar Per Sale** and the **Amount of Purchases Per Month**. Improving just **ONE** of these metrics means positive revenue for your business. What type of impact would that have for your business if you improved a little in all three!

Implementing my evergreen *Beat the Recession* strategy is how you will get there. Realistically I want to imagine what would happen if you increased each metric by just 10%.

Look at the amount of **NEW** revenue that would translate into monthly- a $13,240 increase in sales and $158,880 annually. How's that for results?

This is the type of *IMPACT* putting a system in place can produce. Now these figures really are conservative numbers to play with. Just a **10%** increase in customers (*100 People*), **10%** increase in average sales *($4)*, and **10%** increase in purchases monthly (*1 Visit*). In most cases your numbers will be higher. Either way it goes, improving just **ONE** metric puts you in the green.

The second formula we're going to learn is called "*Advanced ROI*".

ADVANCED ROI:

The *Advanced ROI Formula* is designed to show you how to put both revenue and profit in your pocket. Remember how you learned that having a customer database (*List*) really is the biggest asset any business can possess? Many million dollar companies, like Groupon™, operate solely based on this business model.

	Subscribers (Size of List)		Promotions per month		Response Rate		Avg Dollars per Sale		Monthly Sales Total		Annual Sales Total
Baseline	300	X	4	X	8%	X	$20	=	$1,920	=	$23,040
Size of List	500		700		1000		2000		5000		
Revenue/Month	$ 3,200		$ 4,480		$ 6,400		$ 12,800		$ 32,000		
Percent Discount	25%		25%		25%		25%		25%		
Cost of Discount	$800		$1,120		$1,600		$3,200		$8,000		
Cost of Service	$ -		$ -		$ -		$ -		$ -		
Net Profit/Month	$2,400		$3,360		$4,800		$9,600		$24,000		

What you're going to learn is how profitable building a Customer List for your business can be. Take a look above at our local restaurant example. Let's say my business has built an initial list of 300 prospects.

This list was created from all the marketing methods **(Pillars)** covered inside the course. From that subscriber list you will send out 4 promotions monthly to them. The average response rate from your promotional messages is 8% (*Low*) with $20 being the average customer.

In **Month 1** the revenue produced from starting this kind of campaign would be $1,920 in monthly revenue and $23,040 annually. Similar to the last formula, there are 4 metrics you care about.

1. Subscribers (*Size of List*)
2. Promotions Per Month
3. Response Rate
4. Average Dollar Per Sale

I want you to STOP and look at the $1,920 of new revenue. All this revenue was generated from having a list. This is revenue you didn't have before, but can count on growing monthly.

Let's say the size of your list in month two increases by 100 people. Remember that these aren't buyers, just interested people who joined your list through your company's irresistible offer.

Our monthly revenue in that case would increase to $2,560. Now you can see where this is going. Each month you are steadily growing your list. At some point, your list will start going viral, especially if what you have to offer has high perceived value- targeting your messages to solve consumer's needs, wants and desires.

From this point forward your monthly revenue skyrockets. The amazing fact is your only focused on improving **ONE** metric- the "*Size of the List*". Imagine what will happen if you improve 2 more or **ALL** 4 metrics. Notice how small incremental changes make such a big impact in your business.

The third formula that we're going to discuss is called "*Customer Value*".

CUSTOMER VALUE:

The *Customer Value Formula* is designed to show you the Lifetime Value of EACH customer. Most businesses think the value of a customer is based solely on the dollar amount customers spend, totally *excluding* the number of sales a year and the years EACH customer stays with you.

There's so much money businesses leave on the table, when you don't know everything about your customer.

One good customer can send additional referrals your way. Many of those referrals will become new customers. Understanding the worth of each customer will definitely change how you do business.

Similar to all the other ROI formulas, there are *4 metrics* you want to focus on:

1. **Number of Sales Per Year**
2. **Number of Years a Customer Stays**
3. **Additional Customer Referrals a Year**
4. **Percent of Referrals Who Become Customers**

	Lifetime Value of a Customer		% Increase	
A	Amount of Average Sale	$20	0%	$20
B	No. of Sales per year	24	25%	30.0
C	No. of Years a Customer	3	0%	3
D	Additional Customers Referrals/Year	4	0%	4
E	% of referrals who become customers	50%	25%	63%
F	Gross Sales per Year (A x B)	$480		$600
G	Gross Sales over lifetime (F x C)	$1,440		$1,800
H	New Cutomers Annually from Referrals	2.0		2.5
I	Lifetime Sales from Referrals (H x C x G)	$8,640		$13,500
J	**Total Value of a Loyal Customer (I +G)**	**$10,080**	**52%**	**$15,300**

Let's say for example our local restaurant receives on average $20 per sale. The average customer visits two times a month or 24 times a year. Also the customer continues to visit our restaurant for 3 years.

During this timeframe, each customer refers about four new customers per year, but out of those 4 brand new referral customers, two of them or 50% become reoccurring customers.

Drumroll please, here's the magic. Based on our example, the *Lifetime Customer Value* would be $10,080. WOW! Imagine if every time you saw a new customer. A picture of $10,080 popped into your mind. How would that really impact your company's customer service approach and overall business reputation? For most businesses this impact would be massive.

This is where making very small incremental changes again plays such a BIG part in producing **REAL** Results and **REAL** Revenue. From the power and effectiveness of our *Beat the Recession* campaign, the number of sales per year increases by 25%. That's only 24 sales a year to 30.

Next, the amount of customer referrals increases by just 25%. That's 4 referrals a year to 5. These numbers are very conservative and practical. In this scenario your *Lifetime Customer Value* of each customer would then increase from $10,080 to $15,300 dollars.

These results were made possible by improving just **TWO** metrics. Imagine what would happen if you increased a little in all **FOUR**.

Remember, these powerful metrics already exist inside your business. Improving them will only improve your businesses profitability.

Conclusion:

In closing I hope that you now realize what kind of results having a system in place can produce. I'm trying to eliminate any possible doubt you may have, by showing you **REAL** Proof of how this would actually work. Understanding exactly how your marketing plan directly relates to ROI paints a vivid picture of what type of success you can achieve.

The brilliant thing about all 3 of these formulas is how well they work together; from the **Front End Marketing** (*Sales Booster*) to the **Back End Marketing** (*Advanced ROI & Customer Value Formula*). There's more revenue being created and even more profit being made.

You are leaving absolutely nothing to chance, but revealing a door of endless opportunity. Block out any distractions you may have and go for it. Take **MASSIVE ACTION**. Make a real difference in your business's bottom-line. You deserve it!

Notes

_____

_____

_____

_____

_____

_____

_____

_____

_____

_____

_____

_____

_____

_____

_____

_____

_____

_____

_____

_____

_____

BONUS: "What's My Reputation?"

Welcome to *Beat the Recession Marketing* bonus training on "What's My Reputation?" My main goal during this chapter is to show you step by step how to dominate your market online.

I'm going to give you the edge that your company needs to achieve rock star status in your industry, and position your company as the market leader.

So let's start out by showing you some dramatic shifts that have just happened in the marketplace. I want to do this by reminding you that every day people look online for your products and services.

▢	dentists west palm beach ▾	High	2,400
▢	chiropractor chicago ▾	High	8,100
▢	contractor boston ▾	Medium	4,400
▢	appliance repair denver ▾	High	2,900
▢	realtor orlando ▾	Medium	8,100
▢	electrician charleston ▾	High	720
▢	plumber seattle ▾	High	9,900
▢	pediatrician philadelphia ▾	Low	1,900
▢	locksmith london ▾	High	12,100

In previous chapters, I showed you how to use Google™ to find how the *Modern Consumer* goes about searching for you.

Let's say for example that I needed a Dentist in West Palm Beach, Appliance Repair in Denver, and a Pediatrician in Philadelphia.

In a small city, like West Palm Beach, twenty four hundred people are looking for a Dentist. Look at Denver Appliance Repair- twenty nine hundred, or Pediatrician in Philadelphia- nineteen hundred. I mean the numbers here are mind boggling.

Can you imagine the hundreds, if not thousands, of people online every single month looking for your business? The question is, when they search can they find you? Every day people, as you can see, are looking for businesses and services just like yours.

The next problem consumer's face is: **who** should they do business with and what steps do they take to find the most reputable company to do business with.

Stepping back to understand why a consumer chooses you over the competition creates a question. Would you buy a product or service that has bad ratings and reviews? Ask yourself. Obviously, it would be no! No one wants to actually have that exact same experience when they buy a product or service.

We always look at reviews as the indicator of how we might experience that product or service. But here is the more important question.

Two products are identical; one has ten good reviews; the other has three good reviews, but one bad review. Which one do you buy?

Obviously, the company with ten good reviews-. **WHY** is that? Because you want to have a great experience and you're looking to make sure that a company is **VERY** consistent with delivering that experience or that service.

This is what modern consumers, individuals, and companies do every single day. They go online looking to find the most reputable company to do business with. Just **ONE** bad review can send a customer from your website or your listing online somewhere else. That means a huge difference between your phone ringing and your competition's phone ringing.

I want to talk to you about *Reputation Marketing*. The single most important way you could ever market your business online. Now there are a lot of companies out there that actually do *Reputation Management*.

The main reason I don't believe in reputation management is because reputation management doesn't get a business's phone ringing or attract new customers. Management is a very **defensive posture**. Marketing is a very **offensive posture**. When you see or hear a company doing reputation management, in my opinion that company really doesn't understand the **BIG** picture. What they should be doing is Reputation Marketing. Why is that? Simply because your company's *reputation is everything*! Perception often times is reality in the consumer eyes. More importantly, the way online marketing is played has changed and your competition doesn't even know it.

Every business has been involved in some type of reputation management. Everything from press releases, public appearances, to follow up calls. All of these methods are a form of reputation management. But the mass majority of businesses still don't understand how these **NEW** game changers directly affect their business. Let's talk about these game changers.

Game Changer #1:

In 2012 any company name and city that's entered into a search engine will reveal the company's reputation; For example, perform a search online for any business name, plus their city, and see what comes up.

Following their company name is their reputation score. More importantly, their **Zagat**™ reputation score. This particular company on the next page has 15 out of 30, which is an incredibly poor score. Anyone actually searching for them, even just for directions, is going to see is how bad an online reputation they have. This is incredible!

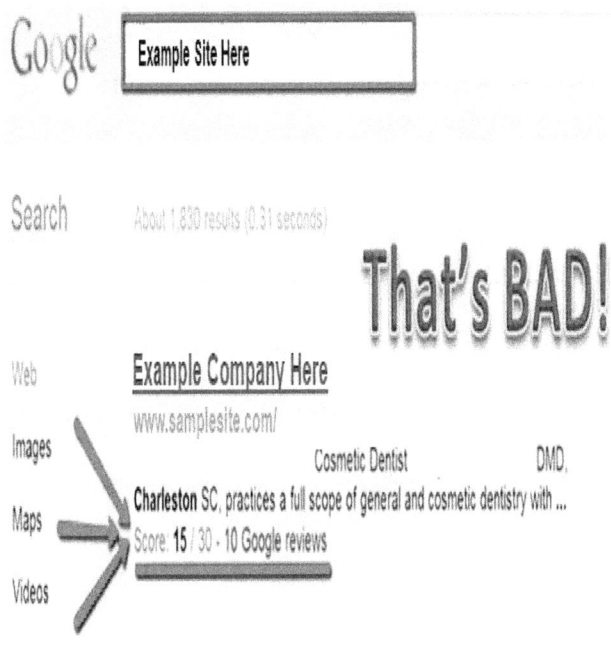

Next I want you to open up an internet browser, type in your company name and see what happens. Before anything comes to the top, I want you to see what is happening.

Search engines are now providing suggestions of what hundreds or even thousands of people have typed in. This is proof positive that people just aren't looking for you, but they are looking for reviews about you.

Now not every company gets these suggestions, but just knowing that you can see that people are actually typing these words is eye opening.

It's a major asset for anybody that wants to do business with you, or even refer people to you, and they want to check you out online to see about your reviews.

Once someone does a search for your company name, the reviews become center stage for the whole world to see. In most cases the reviews are positioned right at the top of search results when someone's actually trying to find your company. These reviews can either help your phone to ring or send interested consumers to your competition.

Very quickly you could see how these **BIG** game changers affect 80 million companies all around the world. Whenever someone types in their name and city into a search engine, their reputation is the first thing people see. It's important when someone types in your name that they find a five-star rating, and many five-star reviews about your company.

Game Changer #2:

Customer social reviews are now a major factor in almost every type of online marketing. When you perform an online search for local information **bad reviews** show up in *Google Maps™*, *Google Plus Listings™* and *Google Pay Per Click™*.

Look at the image on the next page. You can see reviews showing up inside the Pay Per Click, Website Rankings and Organic Rankings.

They also show up in local business directories like *Yelp™, City Search™, Bing™, Yahoo™* and *Yellow Pages™*. Reviews have become a major factor in almost every type of online marketing.

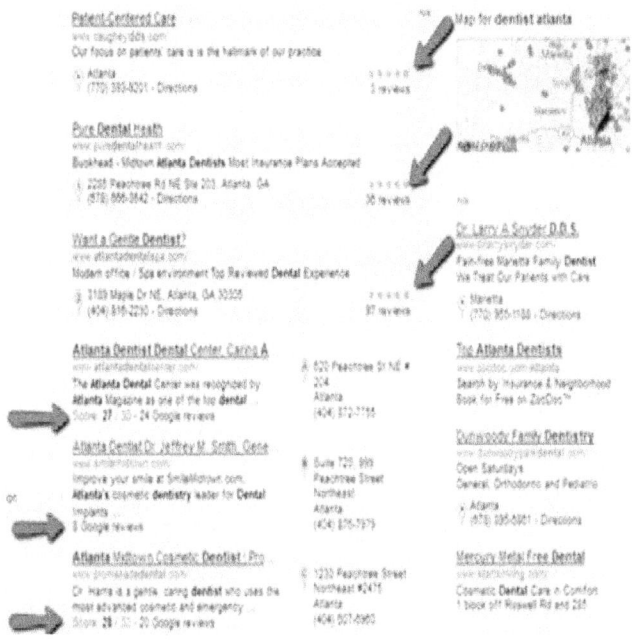

This dramatically affects **ALL** businesses who are currently marketing online; everything from *SEO, Social Media, Pay Per Click to Local Marketing.* Nothing works anymore if you have **bad reviews** or **bad reputation online**.

Why would you want to spend all your time and marketing dollars creating an online presence, only to let consumers find bad reviews? Stop to think about this from the consumer's perspective.

Would you ever buy a product or service from a company that has bad ratings and reviews?

The shift happening right now has taken several years to completely flip-flop the online marketing world, before guarding your online reputation consisted of just *Google Maps™, Yelp™, Video Marketing* and *Blogging*. Then you would work on getting some great reviews or work on getting some customers reviews through Social Media. That's completely the opposite of what today's marketing is about.

Step One requires your business to create a **Five-STAR Reputation first**. After you achieve this, then *Step Two* is investing money into marketing your products and services online or offline.

The reason I suggest this order is to stop you from wasting **HARD** earned money. Think about how modern consumers are researching online looking for the best company with the best reputation that satisfies their needs. Understand the consumer looking for a business with the best reputation is looking for someone to *TRUST*. Creating a Five-Star Reputation for your company positions instant creditability and gets the phone ringing.

Game Changer #3:

We've talked about what's happened kind of negatively with reputation; now let's talk about some positive things when it comes to these changes. The biggest benefit of building a reputation is how good reviews send you prequalified, presold customers, because buyers (*online or offline*) trust reviews as much as personal recommendations. Reviews can be incredibly bad for you if they're bad, but they can be incredibly good for you if they're really good.

In fact statistics show *72% of buyers trust reviews as much as personal recommendations*. If I was to ask a hundred different companies, and let me just ask you. Would you rather create a marketing plan where people *don't know you*, *don't like you*, *don't trust you* and are consistently worried about price? Or would you rather create a marketing plan where people *know you*, *like you* and *trust you* plus they're all referrals? Well, for the first time in history online marketing can be just as powerful as referral marketing. Because three out of four people now trust reviews just as much as personal recommendations.

Hopefully, you can see how powerful having five star reviews on your listings is for business. In the real world it's similar to someone's mother saying "*you should buy from this company*" or your best friend saying "*you should use this type of service, I've used it*".

This type of personal endorsement speaks higher than any form of marketing could ever do. Why? Simply because these reviews are unbiased and honestly tell the truth of how good or bad the quality of service rendered was. Let's really dig deeper into this fact. For inside this game changer *alone* is enough power to change your business!

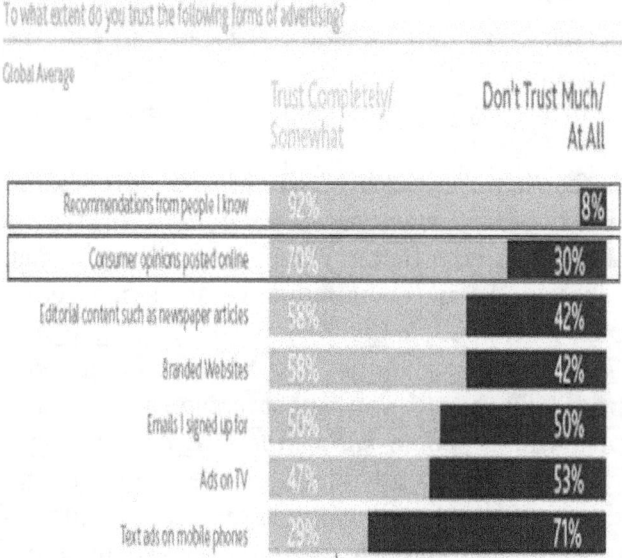

To what extent do you trust the following forms of advertising?

Global Average	Trust Completely/ Somewhat	Don't Trust Much/ At All
Recommendations from people I know	92%	8%
Consumer opinions posted online	70%	30%
Editorial content such as newspaper articles	58%	42%
Branded Websites	58%	42%
Emails I signed up for	50%	50%
Ads on TV	47%	53%
Text ads on mobile phones	29%	71%

Source: Nielsen Global Trust In Advertising Survey, Q3 2011

Recently a survey conducted by Nielsen Global Trust™ reported the top rated companies in the world when it comes to advertising. The survey explained to what extent consumers trust different forms of advertising, and which are the most important things that they trust.

Amazingly, 92% of people trust recommendations from people that they know. But here's the BIG one. Look below at the one right under that. Seventy percent trust opinions based on **online reviews**. This is huge!

It's extremely important you understand prospects actually *TRUST* consumer opinions posted online more than an editorial newspaper or article. You could actually have a newspaper article written about you that is editorial and people will not trust that as much as an online review.

All the evidence from here forward points to the fact that: *Reputation Marketing* is the **MOST** important marketing that someone could do for their business. If you going to inject any type of marketing plan into your business, make sure it doesn't **START** with the type of marketing that people don't trust like: *TV Ads at 47%* or *E-mail Marketing at 50%* or even *Branded Website Marketing at 58%.*

It should start with the top two recommendations from "**people that people know**" and "**consumer opinions posted online**" which is *Reputation Marketing*.

Why is reputation so vital to a business?

Reputation Marketing strongly appeals to how our human psyche operates. The modern consumer looks up an average of 10 reviews before making a decision. Remember, the majority of these consumers are online looking for you and reading the online reviews. More importantly, they're looking at multiple reviews, not just one or two. Stats show *70% of consumers trust a business with a minimum of 6-10 reviews.* A business today is not seen credible from the consumer perspective, without any five-star reviews. In this social economy we live in, without a five-star reputation and a minimum of ten reviews, in the consumer eyes businesses can't be trusted. This is why marketing is **all about the relationship**.

Slowly the recession has changed how consumers connect with business and research information. When consumers now are trying to find you, the difference between your phone ringing and it not ringing *is your reputation*. More importantly, this is the difference between *your phone not ringing* and *your competition's phone ringing non-stop*. Super important, make sure your business has ten Five-Star Reviews, so when people look for your business online, your phone rings.

What exactly is reputation marketing?

We referenced a bit earlier about how reputation management is kind of the old way of doing business. If you really want to dominate your market, it's all about *Reputation Marketing*. The short breakdown behind *Reputation Marketing* goes something like this. Position your company as the market leader in front of thousands of buyers, with simply a five-star reputation.

It's all about building a five-star reputation online *first* and then going out marketing that reputation. You just learned why this is the MOST Powerful and MOST Trusted type of marketing that any business can do.

How do you create a reputation marketing strategy?

I'm really excited to share this next part with you. One of the first things you need to do is really understand everything about your reputation. So let me ask you. Do you know your reputation online? Do you know what people are saying about you right now?

Well, my clients do and that's the difference. You're not just building a five-star reputation; you're leveraging it and marketing it. The first step is knowing what people are saying about you. When it comes to an online reputation, you're going to find there are really only four types possibly to have.

One is going to be a ***Bad Reputation***. Obviously, you know that that's not good and you're going to need to do something about that fast. Then there's ***No Reputation*** at all, which you just saw, is just as good as having a bad reputation because it doesn't get your phone ringing. You need at least ten positive five-star reviews for you to even look credible online.

Next there's a ***Good Reputation***, and if you have a good reputation that simply means you have some good reviews and maybe a few not so good reviews. If you had to choose between a company with multiple good reviews and one bad review versus another company, who would you go with? My point is having a good review isn't enough. These types of reputations I just explained are not going to get your phone ringing. Your business deserves to be positioned as the industry leader. Creating a *Five-Star Reputation* is going to make you the industry leader.

Here are some insider strategies of how I do it for my clients. Step one- you want to *Develop That Five-Star Reputation* online. Step two- *Market Your Five-Star Reputation* everywhere possible. I'm going to show you exactly how I actually use and leverage the power of this reputation. Broadcasting it out into the marketplace to get people really excited about doing business with your company.

Step three, you want to *Manage That Reputation* and keep that positive reputation going, because you're only *ONE* customer away from a bad review. I mean, everybody has a bad day: the receptionist, your sales person, the person you've hired to fulfill all the products, your strategic partner. Everybody is one day and just one customer away from a bad review. So you want to make sure to manage your reputation.

The last thing you want to do, which is most important is that you want to *Create a Reputation Marketing Culture.* This is extremely fun to do!

It's not enough just to try to fix things, but you want to be proactive inside your business to make sure that every single person in your company is on the same page. Everyone needs to stay motivated to do one thing, provide a great job for your customers and provide them with first-class service. This is mandatory to keep that five-star reputation going. So you can see when you have a plan like this put together, you can dominate your market online.

Now, let's take a look at my first strategy on *Developing That Five-Star Reputation*. There's a lot of ways to accomplish this. One of the best ways that you do this starts off with creating professionally designed review postcards. This may include irresistible offers, coupons, etc. We design these for our clients, and they send them out to their customers. My clients then start receiving appreciation calls and five-star reviews. Another thing that I do is build review business cards. Your staff needs to be armed with a way for your customers to actually give you reviews. Providing them a company business card that tells them where they can put the review, is truly vital for creating a five-star reputation.

I also create personalized email templates for my clients. Emails are a very easy way to get reviews and combined with video works like gangbusters. The only challenges you face is creating a specific type of template that really **"DRAWS"** people to take action. These are proven steps that I do for my clients every day. There are so many more strategies, but these are three that you can apply to your business right away.

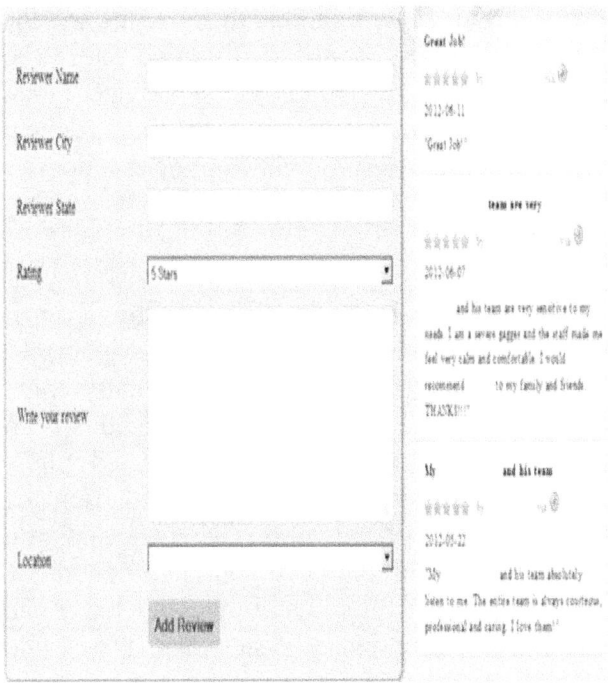

One of the bigger insider strategies I use for my clients is creating private review pages. This can be done on your company website. What you want to have is a one-stop shop for customers to post their reviews. Think about like this. Would you rather someone post a review on Yelp™ that's NOT so good or would you rather them put it in your own personal review website where that review is seen by you first? Well, that's what we do.

We create a private review page, so that all of the reviews are funneled into one area. Then when we receive a review, we can post them online and the only ones we post are the really good ones. The ones that aren't so good, get a private email making sure that our clients can address them before customers post a review online that doesn't reflect a five-star reputation.

Installing a posting review strategy for your business is critical. Let me explain why. Even if you we're to collect these reviews for yourself, businesses can't post reviews that actually come from real customers. The reason behind this is all these different review sites have created filters that delete any reviews that are posted from the same computer IP network. That means if you take a few reviews and have your staff post them, they instantly get filtered and even deleted. I had to develop a proprietary system and process to post reviews for a company without being filtered or defeated.

When you have a private review page you will be able to collect all your reviews and filter them. Having a proprietary system to post the reviews, is the **knockout punch** to dominating your market online and really separating yourself from everyone else in the industry. Let's talk for a few minutes about how to actually market your online reputation. Once you actually built a five-star reputation, how do you actually market it?

The 6 New Reputation Horsemen

If you think that text reviews or reviews posted to a website are powerful, then you should try the first horseman *Video Review Marketing*. The videos I create for my clients are incredible. They literally convert like crazy. Remember the power of video you learned during *Beat the Recession* training? Creating a system and process that captures video reviews is something we love to do with our clients. It's incredibly effective.

Another awesome way to market your five-star reputation and second horseman is *Website Marketing*. Let me ask you, do you have reviews on the front page of your website right now? Well, that's the most powerful thing that you could be doing, injecting instant social proof. I actually post the latest reviews to all our clients' websites. So when someone shows up at that website, they are quickly converted by having an unbelievable user experience.

The third horseman of reputation is *Social Media Marketing*. You know how powerful social media is, but no one really can convert social media into leads until now. When you're using reputation marketing inside your social media campaigns, it becomes incredibly viral.

Next is **Maps Marketing**. We talked a little bit earlier about when someone types in a keyword they're looking for you. Are you the one that's top on the map? More importantly, are you the one with the great reputation? Remember, they may find you and they may find your competition, but the company they're looking to do business with, has the **BEST** reputation.

Moving forward to the fifth horsemen of reputation **Email Marketing**. Remember what you learned when you looked at those Neilson stats; email marketing wasn't really that effective, but when combined with reputation marketing WOW! Every time you send an offer, every time you tell them about a discount or whenever you send out any newsletters type of email. You must couple it with your five-star reputation. It's going to be incredibly powerful if you do.

Last element inside the reputation horsemen is **Sales Marketing**. Companies that take advantage of this concept can literally double their sales conversions. Just imagine the ability to sit in front of a customer that's on the fence of whether they should go with you or buy your competitions products or services. Then you say:

"don't take my word for it: let's go online to see what other customers who are just like you, and see what they thought about working with us".

You'll leave them in amazement as you read all your company's five-star reviews right in front of them. Remember, statistically speaking, that's just as powerful as having their best friend or family member or a colleague at work recommending your products and services to that customer. So you're going to be able to close a lot more sales if you arm yourself with reputation marketing.

How to Manage Your Five-Star Reputation

The proper way to manage your reputation is making sure you monitor it daily. There are a lot of small businesses that actually monitor their branding by using tools like Google Alerts™.

Google Alerts™ is great and so are the hundreds of other tools. But they're not designed for monitoring your reputation. These search engine tools only work when someone types in your name or post something about your product. It searches the entire web for your name or your product name or the name of the CEO. Our only problem with that is when someone posts a review; they're typically doing it on your listing via *Yelp™, City Search™, Bing™, Yahoo™ or Google™.* They just post something about you, but **NOT** your name, **NOT** the CEO's name and **NOT** the products name. So, you can have all the alerts you want from all these tools, but none of them will show you reviews.

Understanding how these tools work is the key. I've had to develop a proprietary system that monitors all the major sites and listings. Every single day I know exactly who posts and what's posted to these sites. Your business must have a similar system in place. Staying on top of your reputation is the overall secret to your success. Every two weeks, I create a report and give it to my clients. I want them to see how their reputation is increasing online.

More importantly, this report is incredible to share with your staff. So the staff know how good they are doing. I post the good reviews and bad reviews in this report. What's more important about that is you can also share with your staff the bad reviews and formulate a plan on how to correct that. It's important to get the entire business on board when it comes to your online marketing.

Another thing you can do and I do for clients are setting up daily review alerts. Whenever there's a negative review posted, you need to know about it. Daily review alerts allow all negative reviews to be sent to a specific department or person in your company so that they can address them immediately, along with positive reviews. On the other hand, when you get a positive review you want to know about that, don't you? In a similar fashion you want to send that to someone else in your company, so they may be able to follow up with that person and even get a referral from it.

Now, managing your reputation isn't just about monitoring or reporting. It's also about continuing to grow your reviews. I work with my clients to continually get them the latest five-star reviews, because your customers don't want to actually see reviews that are six-months, a year, even 18 months old. They want to see up-to-date reviews, to know that you are continually giving great service in the marketplace.

Finally, manage your reputation by marketing only the five-star reviews. This is extremely important because even an average review, even though it's good, isn't going to convert very well unless it has the right information. The correct social and buying triggers must be properly laid out inside of it. That's why I encourage you to continually monitor your reputation for the right reviews. Then post them on your website and all over the web in order to market your reputation online.

The most important thing you need to do while implementing a reputation marketing strategy is creating a *Reputation Marketing Culture* inside your business. So here's the question. You expect your staff to give first-class service to every single one of your customers, right? Well, what's your plan to inspire your staff to give that first-class service to customers and get raving reviews?

What you want to do is actually build a *conscious* reputation marketing culture, so all of your staff is on the same page. Train you staff accordingly and explain everything you expect from them. Show them all the details that your daily reports and reviews reveal, so they can visual understand your vision.

Providing superior customer service and a great user experience is the reason you're going to get customers in the door. This is the most important ingredient for converting leads, dominating your market and really getting that phone to ring with NEW business.

Every company needs a reputation strategy. Your business reputation is **EVERYTHING**! Put a *Reputation Marketing* plan in place *TODAY* that educates consumers WHY your company is the BEST.

RESOURCES

Understand Your Market Tools:

Market Evaluation Keywords Form -
http://goo.gl/Cd6B8

Market Questions & Needs Locator Form -
http://goo.gl/AKcUN

Customer Social Profile - http://goo.gl/f24Tp

Google Keyword Tool - http://goo.gl/K7XFJ

Google Insights/Trends Tool -
http://goo.gl/rSDVF

Quantcast Demographics Tool -
http://goo.gl/QkO4z

Knowing Your Competition Tools:

Competition Website Analysis & Social Analysis
Form - http://goo.gl/jt34L

Traffic Travis - http://goo.gl/qS7Fc

Shared Count - http://goo.gl/Ghmkv

Customer Avatar Discovery Tools:

Ideal Customer "Avatar" Form -
http://goo.gl/hmYKW

Beat The Recession Marketing Extras:

Beat The Recession Blueprint -
http://goo.gl/Z90yD

Visionary ROI Calculator - http://goo.gl/CfZQW

Done 4 You Service (FREE Audit) -
http://goo.gl/11gfr

Beat The Recession BONUS Extras:

Beat The Recession Video Training -
http://goo.gl/kICQy

"What's My Reputation" Video Training -
http://goo.gl/ObzP2

"Why 2 Go Mobile" Video Training -
http://goo.gl/SbjZF

Additional Recession Tools:

Hootsuite - http://goo.gl/l8LhM

SEO Cockpit - http://goo.gl/25AkO
Bomb Bomb Video Email - http://goo.gl/c7WjQ

Aweber - http://goo.gl/jumde

Word Tracker Question Tool -
http://goo.gl/NXWkh

ABOUT THE AUTHOR

James Carley is the CEO/Founder of Visionary Concepts Marketing located in San Diego and Los Angeles, California. He has been mentioned as one of the world's most influential and innovative marketing visionaries.

His ability to understand the modern consumers buying behavior really is amazing. He teaches businesses how to develop winning relationships with their customers that translate into positive marketing ROI.

The main objective of James is helping Small Businesses beat the recession by showing them how to reach customers where they are and how to think like a Marketer. Truly he connects businesses with consumers and consumers with businesses.

His out the box thought process helps position businesses to get MORE Customers, MORE Revenue and MORE Profits. James reveals that SUCCESS isn't magic, it's a process and being a visionary means your only limitation, is your vision.

INDEX

Sales Funnel: is a designated sales process that you send ALL new and interested prospects through. This process allows you to better qualify potential customers in advance while installing Know, Like and Trust factors.

Lead Nurturing: is the process of relationship building after a prospect enters into your sales funnel. This process provides prospects with valuable content that educates, engages and pre-qualifies them for conversions.

Lead Capturing: is the process of directing prospects to a specific location where they can get more information or irresistible offer in exchange for their contact information via Email or Mobile.

Conversion: is the process of getting consumers to respond to marketing messages and perform a desired action. A conversion is simply getting consumers to respond to your Call-To-Actions.

Customer Retention: refers to keeping clients coming back for future business instead of losing them to your competitors' products or services-building a loyal relationship between consumers and your brand.

Online Reputation: refers to how consumers view your business based solely on their user experience. Very similar to word-of-mouth, a good reputation helps presale new customers and increases referral growth.

Marketing Channel: is the process of how businesses present their products to targeted users. Also called distribution channels which for the modern consumer are often times online.

Multi-Channel Marketing: is marketing your products or services using many different marketing channels to reach a customer. Being present wherever the modern consumer interacts.

Optimization: is setting up and structuring all of your online or offline marketing efforts to receive maximum results. Developing and Structuring all current marketing channels to convert prospects into a desired outcome (*sale, call, click, etc.*).

FrontEnd Marketing: is the process of focusing all marketing activity & promotions on customer acquisition. Finding creative ways to attract new prospects into your company sales funnel.

BackEnd Marketing: is the strategic process of generating new business from past or existing customers. Finding creative ways to encourage and motivate previous customers to come back for repeat business.

Customer Avatar: is the visual representation of "what" you're markets Ideal customer looks like. Understanding this allows your marketing to directly speak the language of your consumer and become relevant.

Demographics: are certain key elements that describe detailed information about "WHO" your ideal customer is including age, race, sex, levels of education and current income level.

Barrier Of Entry: represents all the challenges and obstacles businesses face when entering into a particular market. These hindrances can include price objections, product information, fierce competition or blocked marketing channels.

Data Mining: is the process of discovering useful information from large data sets (*applications, customer files, receipts, etc.*). Extracting quality information and giving it useful meaning for future projects.

Reverse Engineering: is the process of taking apart an object to understand how it works in order to emulate that object or improve upon it.

BackLinks: are incoming links to a webpage from various web properties that represent a vote. Similar to an election these backlinks signify to search engines people are talking about this website.

Business Metrics: is any type of measurement being used to gauge a business's return on investment (*ROI*) and find areas of improvement.

Shareability: refers to how easy information is shared socially or between individuals both online and offline.

Social Proof: is the hidden force that influences consumers when faced with purchasing decisions. This influential power is directly connected to the psychology of how and why consumers buy.

Social Integration: is the action of creating your brands presence across all popular social media platforms. Properly making sure consumers either online or offline can easily "join the conversation" socially.

Relevant: refers to the process in which brands understand their consumer's needs, wants and frustrations. Then being able to accurately deliver solutions that satisfy their ideal customer.

Optins: is the process when a consumer has given permission for a business to send them promo text messages or emails. This normally happens when a modern consumer signs up for discounts, online products or coupons.

ROI: stands for Return On Investment for profit generated from all marketing investments. ROI can determine if a campaign was successful or a complete failure. Ultimately revealing what exact marketing channels are really working for your business.

Competition Reports: are detailed spreadsheets that contain all the information about your Market and Competitors. Revealing the clues or roadmap that a business must follow to become visible in the marketplace.

Landing Page: is a dedicated Web or Mobile page that easily allows a business to capture a consumer's contact information, through a lead capture form.

Targeted Consumers: is a group of customers that have shown interest in a company's products or services. Marketing to targeted consumers is the first step in developing a custom marketing strategy.

Syndication: is the process of taking all of your online content such as articles, videos or images and making them available on multiple online platforms (*social networks, blogs, bookmarks*).

Law Of Reciprocity: is based around the golden principle of giving or doing something of value and that goodwill coming back to you. This principle is behind "WHY" a business provides something of value (*product or service*) and their business receives new sales as a direct result.

www.ingramcontent.com/pod-product-compliance
Lightning Source LLC
Chambersburg PA
CBHW051528170526
45165CB00002B/652